MISSION IMPOSSIBLE?

The Power of The Gemini Way

VICTORIA R. BONDOC

Disclaimer:

The author strives to be as accurate and complete as possible in the creation of this book, notwithstanding the fact that the author does not warrant or represent at any time that the contents within are accurate due to the rapidly changing nature of the Internet.

While all attempts have been made to verify information provided in this publication, the Author and the Publisher assume no responsibility and are not liable for errors, omissions, or contrary interpretation of the subject matter herein. The Author and Publisher hereby disclaim any liability, loss or damage incurred as a result of the application and utilization, whether directly or indirectly, of any information, suggestion, advice, or procedure in this book. Any perceived slights of specific persons, peoples, or organizations are unintentional.

In practical advice books, like anything else in life, there are no guarantees of income made. Readers are cautioned to rely on their own judgment about their individual circumstances to act accordingly. Readers are responsible for their own actions, choices, and results. This book is not intended for use as a source of legal, business, accounting or financial advice. All readers are advised to seek the services of competent professionals in legal, business, accounting, and finance field.

Printed in the United States of America

ISBN: 978-1-948382-19-9 paperback
JMP2021.3

To my parents Remedios Rosales Bondoc, M.D.,
and Conrado C. Bondoc, M.D.

I was a big challenge.
I was your maverick. And I was your risk-taker.

When you thought I was abandoning an MIT degree
in mathematics and a good engineering job to start
Gemini, you told your friends, "I don't understand
what she does . . . I just know it's a *Secret*."

When things got tough,
you came up with a million ideas to help.

And when I went to Panama to work with
the Army investigating black market crime,
you prayed every night until I returned.

You gave me many gifts. You gave me the education,
the strength, and the confidence to do anything.
Gemini's thirty-five-year commitment and
National Security contribution are your success
as much as Gemini's or mine.

Today I have an amazing family that includes
not only your children, grandchildren, and their
children, but also a *Gemini Family*. Although they
are extraordinary, loyal, and give me strength,
I miss you every minute of every day.

CONTENTS

FOREWORD

Meeting Victoria Bondoc is like coming face to face with an indomitable force of nature. She radiates energy and imagination. She's a classic example of an executive for whom the impossible does not exist. It's a goal to be done immediately, conceding that miracles take a little longer.

Anyone who fails to recognize that her strong parents, Remedios Rosales Bondoc, M.D., and Conrado C. Bondoc, M.D., make a difference need look no farther than Ms. Bondoc for enlightenment. Being the child of two physicians would seem to give her a leg up on life. Actually, her success required surmounting the huge obstacle of being legally blind. But she learned from her parents, both immigrants from the Philippines, the values of hard work, discipline, and the imperative to excel—and to inspire anyone she comes into contact to excel. Her parents survived the trauma of the Japanese occupation of their native nation, which she captures in a snapshot that defines the harrowing reality of what evil looks and behaves like.

They infused their daughter with enthusiasm, optimism, and the confidence that she could achieve any goal to which she set her mind. She earned a degree in Mathematics from the Massachusetts Institute of Technology and landed a good engineering job. But she set her goals higher.

And what a goal she settled upon. The U.S. defense industry is dominated by men. Naturally, she decided to found not just a defense industry company, but one that would gain national and international recognition for outstanding performance, innovation, and the drive to stay on the cutting edge of technology and the deployment of human resources. For her, it all starts with character and values. In character, expressed through values of integrity, hard work, loyalty, and commitment to excellence, there is power.

In 1986, she founded Gemini, today one of the defense industries' most respected companies, in the belief that the right positive mindset enables you to overcome any obstacle. Her high impact, results-oriented leadership proved she knew how to get things done. She thinks big and she delivers big. What defines results for a dynamic leader like this?

When the U.S. Military launched OPERATION ENDURING FREEDOM in Afghanistan, she overcame doubters and forged a program using local resources to cut delivery time of critical equipment and materials from six months to two weeks. When Improvised Explosive Devices threatened safety and lives of our men and women in uniform, she propelled a Gemini intelligence team to complete 24,000 intelligence tasks that halted terrorist activities and clamped down on IED assaults. Products her team generated helped identify and capture the Boston Marathon bombing suspects.

Ms. Bondoc leads and inspires the men and women who make Gemini the stand-out story of achievement for a team that makes a habit of not only living up to but exceeding what's expected of them. The team itself shines because they share the view that failure is not an option. As Ms. Bondoc declares: Mission Success cannot be impossible. It's something Gemini's team will achieve. She sums up the impact on clients and that her own team has upon one another once a task is completed: WOW. That's what success requires to become a bright, shining star in handling complex, high-priority National Security challenges. In her words, the team applies an "All-In approach and a No-Fail, No-Excuses performance standard to ensure that each customer is a Winner."

The Gemini team she built knows that they stand for something larger than the contributions of any individual. They take pride in beating the odds, to conquer Mission Impossible. Victoria Bondoc's approach stresses the importance of thinking and acting like a winner. She articulates key steps for achieving success: picture the win. Keep score. Have the courage to succeed. Persevere. Put in the work and planning. Choose to overcome any obstacle. Make decisions that maximize the four elements of success: potential, action, results, and attitude. She's forged that mantra into The Gemini Way.

This fine book expresses her engaging, fascinating mind, relentless energy, passion to lead from the front and to inspire those she works with to share in Gemini's success and the triumphs that are marks of great leadership. As you read this book, you're invited to see how her dynamic mindset turns Gemini into a national leader—a top performer whose success was earned through its innovative ideas to solve problems, rapid response and proactive support for clients, and high-impact, successful delivery of on-time results.

Victoria Bondoc launched her current success at age 25. People viewed her as a longshot — the darkest of dark horses. She proved to be a shining star. Her peers recognized that when her leadership stood out as a role model to respect and follow. At Gemini, today she is the CEO of an inspirational, growing enterprise whose achievements earned it recognition as the Aerospace and Defense Company of the Year.

This book is a joy to read, and the lessons she learned are ones that are worth heeding. In her call to arms, she advises the reader: "You are ready to face the challenges . . . what are you waiting for?" Well stated, true, and a beacon that lights the road on the way ahead.

James P. Farwell
Associate Fellow, Department of War Studies,
Kings College, University of London;
non-resident Senior Fellow,
The Middle East Institute, Washington, D.C.,
Author of *Persuasion & Power and Information Warfare*

ACKNOWLEDGMENTS

April 23, 2021, marks the 35th Anniversary of Gemini Industries Inc. in National Security.

I am proud of Gemini's All-In approach, *No-Fail, No-Excuses* performance standard, and the achievements of Gemini teams on complex, high-priority National Security projects. They have supported program execution, advanced technology, intelligence, planning, and operations. They have delivered tools to help U.S. forces apprehend terrorists. And they have reviewed foreign actions that threaten the U.S.

Our National Security depends on the men and women who serve in Defense, State, and Homeland Security positions around the world. Their skill, courage, and dedication make *Mission Success* possible. I am very grateful for their sacrifice.

It has been a privilege to support the efforts of Defense, Homeland Security, Transportation, Commerce, and State.

I am particularly grateful to Defense and Homeland Security leaders who gave me the opportunity to contribute to their team:

Mr. James Guerts, Assistant Secretary of the Navy for Research, Development and Acquisition

Mr. John B. Salvatori, Director, Secretary of the Air Force, Concepts, Development, & Management Office

Brigadier General Edward L. Mahan, (U.S. Air Force, Retired) Vice Commander, Air Force Materiel Command, Electronics Systems Center

Mr. Paul Sturm (Senior Executive Service, Retired) Chief of Staff, Counter-IED Operations/Intelligence Integration Center, Joint IED Defeat Organization

Mr. James W. Cluck (Senior Executive Service, Retired) Acquisition Executive, Department of Defense

Finally, the family members of each member of the Gemini team deserve special thanks. They encourage us. They are patient when National Security priorities need our time. And they say "Get OVER yourself" when we need to hear it. Gemini cannot do what must be done without their generosity, time, and support.

LIST OF ABBREVIATIONS AND TERMS

A-B-Cs of the battlefield	Attention to detail, Big decisions, and the courage to make them, Credibility
ASD	Advanced Solutions Division
BLUF	Bottom Line Up Front
CEO	Chief Executive Officer
COVID-19	Coronavirus disease 2019
C3I	Command, Control, Communications, and Intelligence
C4ISR	Command, Control, Communications, Computers, Intelligence, Surveillance, and Reconnaissance
Hold the Line	Maintain the existing position or state of affairs. The phrase alludes to former military tactics, in which a line of troops was expected to prevent an enemy breakthrough.

ICON	Invest in success, Create a "Yes, if" Strategy, Open-up, Never be late.
IED	Improvised Explosive Device
Incoming	A warning that something (such as enemy fire) is coming toward you
IMS	Integrated Master Schedule
ISO	International Organization for Standardization
JIDO	Joint Improvised-Threat Defeat Organization
Mission Success	Successfully complete objectives within the required timeframe
Navy SEAL	Navy Sea, Air and Land
NORAD	North American Aerospace Defense Command
OEF	Operation Enduring Freedom
PARAMAX	Potential, Action, Results, Attitude—to the MAX.
Return Fire	Doing what is required to protect yourself if you have been fired on, or otherwise attacked
RPM	Results-focused Priority-driven Mission Plans
SITREP	Situation Report

SOF	Special Operations Forces
Take High Ground	Holding the high ground offers an elevated vantage point with a wide field of view and surveillance of the surrounding landscape

INTRODUCTION

Do you miss the excitement of looking at the future and seeing so many opportunities that are there for the taking?

You felt it at your High School Graduation. It was strong on the first day of a new job. And it peaked at the start of that important, difficult, and maybe even dangerous assignment that only you could do.

After a year of frustration, disappointment, and uncertainty it is easy to put things off. It is easy to focus on fear. And it is easy to settle for *good enough*.

What if your life could be an exciting adventure filled with energy, optimism, and reward? Starting the adventure takes courage; and building momentum takes discipline and commitment. Isn't a more exciting life worth the effort?

You can get back the confidence to create solutions. You can feel the energy pressing you to do more. And you can produce results that will change your life.

Facing *Mission Impossible*

The United States is the world leader because of its dynamic economy, network of allies, and military strength. Extraordinary individuals work long hours to execute the actions necessary to further U.S. interests and respond to National Security threats. Their skill, sacrifice, and accomplishments build on the foundation created by millions of patriots who came before us, to sustain our strength and global leadership.

National Security leaders are responsible for important programs. They face *Mission Impossible* every day. They must make decisions that affect the strength of the United States and the safety of more than 325 million people who live in the country. They must successfully complete objectives within the required timeframe. In other words, they must have *Mission Success*.

I started Gemini Industries Inc. and grew the company to specialize in high-priority National Security challenges and an All-In approach to ensure customer *Mission Success.*

This book is a tribute to the Gemini team. Gemini has worked on projects around the globe. Project teams create solutions that affect the lives of people. The goals are tough, and the schedules are tight. They tackle issues that many describe as complex and some call *impossible.* And they deliver the strategic, technological, and operational solutions to ensure *Mission Success.*

This book is also a force multiplier to increase performance to higher and higher levels. My customers are among the brightest and most respected individuals in the country. The Gemini approach is directed to their priorities and decisions. The commitment of the Gemini team to their customer is uncompromising. And *Mission Success* is first and foremost the direct result of the customer's leadership.

Understanding the power and potential of *The Gemini Way* is critical to the future. It instills the optimism to set bold goals. It brings focus, energy, and tools. And it gives you the strength to persevere until you overcome obstacles.

This book honors the success of the Gemini team and *The Gemini Way* that will continue to turn *Mission Impossible* to *Mission Success* in the years ahead.

Fuse your power with external forces to achieve goals

The future is full of possibilities and opportunities if you have the courage to set a big, bold, or wild goal.

Evan Spiegel, Ludwig van Beethoven, and General George Washington have something in common:

- Evan Spiegel created *Snapchat* with Bobby Murphy and Reggie Brown while they were students, and at age twenty-five, he became a billionaire and one of the youngest CEOs of a publicly traded company.

- Ludwig van Beethoven was the predominant musical figure in the transitional period between the Classical and Romantic eras, despite his increasing and eventual deafness.

- General George Washington led a poorly trained and undersupplied Continental Army through six years of struggle and setbacks to defeat Britain and win the War for Independence.

They are champions from different walks of life. And they all started right where *you* are now.

This book will show you how to seize the power of character to advance your skills. You will learn to build resources to strengthen your power. And you will see how to fuse the power of decision, momentum, and perception to persevere through difficult times and succeed.

Maybe that dream is within reach. Once you set your sights on it, the excitement of the possibility of that goal will push you to action. You will find new energy chasing what is possible and enjoy the adventure.

The Gemini Way can help anyone

The power of *The Gemini Way* is not limited to National Security. It is not limited to the highly educated or the wealthy. It can help anyone:

- Teams facing challenges
- People who want to break into an environment dominated by a different economic or cultural group
- Women working in a male-dominated field
- People with a physical disability

I was born with a handicap that left me legally blind. Using *The Gemini Way*, I built a multimillion-dollar business in National Security. Today I lead a team of extraordinary professionals who apply the same principles to create innovative solutions to complex challenges.

So, I know that it can work for you, because it worked for me and for my team for thirty-five years.

Don't delay doing the *Impossible*

You can face your challenges now. Learn how to overcome the impossible.

There's no time for delay, today is the day.

Let's go!

CHAPTER 1

Today Is the Day

The *American Dream* is the belief that anyone in the United States can achieve success through hard work.

The opportunity and freedom that America offers has inspired so many to pursue their goals, raise a family, and prosper. And their success has contributed to the strength of a country that is the undisputed world leader.

Today, America's strength comes from its military, network of allies, and a dynamic economy. Our military is the greatest in history, with the best troops, training, and technology. Our commitment to diplomacy has created a network of alliances that strengthens our defense and contributes to our progress through challenging times. American businesses and workers consistently outperform anyone in the world. And entrepreneurs start exciting new businesses every day.

The United States is the world leader because of the efforts of talented professionals who are committed to exceptional performance. More than 2 million men and women in the Armed Forces serve in 160 countries and protect our freedoms. Two hundred forty thousand aviation, border security, emergency response, cybersecurity, and chemical facility inspector professionals keep America safe. And more than 75,000 men and women within the State Department work to strengthen our priorities at embassies, consulates, and offices across the globe.

They have extraordinary talent and work long hours to execute the actions necessary to respond to National Security threats, to further U.S. interests, and to strengthen the country. Their sacrifice and accomplishments build on the foundation created by millions of patriots who came before to sustain our strength and global leadership.

Today is the day that you can decide to apply talent and energy creating a bigger, bolder, and better future.

Could we lose our freedom?

Achieving the impossible did not start with me. It began with my parents, Remedios Rosales Bondoc, M.D., and Conrado C. Bondoc, M.D.

My parents came to America in 1960 and were naturalized as U.S. citizens.

They were born and raised in the Republic of the Philippines. Both pursued a career in medicine. My father chose to become a surgeon. My mother specialized in neurology and neuropathology.

They emigrated to the U.S. in 1960 and worked hard to heal the sick and raise a family.

They told us stories about life in the Philippines during World War II.

On December 8, 1941, Japan invaded the Philippines. Clark Air Base in Pampanga and Nichols Field outside Manila were attacked. On December 22, the Japanese forces landed at the Lingayen Gulf and continued to Manila.

Manila was occupied by the Japanese on January 2, 1942. General Douglas MacArthur retreated with his troops to Bataan while the commonwealth government withdrew to Corregidor Island before proceeding to the United States. The joint American and Filipino soldiers in Bataan finally surrendered on April 9, 1942.

Many things in the Philippines changed during the three-year occupation by Japan. Clocks in the Philippines were changed to Tokyo time. Currency was modified. And all law schools and many medical schools were closed. Armed soldiers were stationed across urban and rural areas, and Filipinos were required to bow when meeting a Japanese soldier. Those who failed to bow were slapped until respect was properly paid.

I will never forget their stories of the three-year occupation. Japanese soldiers used powerful symbols to control the population. My father told me that the mayor of the town was forced to consume an object that was attached to a long wire. The object passed through his digestive system and was excreted. Both ends of the wire were secured to suspend the Mayor at the center of the town. Even worse, the Mayor was suspended at a height that forced him to remain on his toes in order to limit damage to internal organs and minimize physical pain. The public display was a shocking sight and a warning to any who might dare to challenge the rule of Imperial Japan.

*Philippine currency changed to reflect
the rule of Imperial Japan.*

When Imperial Japan surrendered in 1945, Japanese soldiers set fires as they retreated. My mother's family could only watch as their home burned to the ground. They walked from house to house, as each was set on fire, carrying the only items they would have to rebuild their lives.

I could sense my parents' frustration at the misfortune of life. I could hear their sadness from the loss of those who did not survive. And I could feel the anger that remained after more than twenty years.

Their stories gave me great respect for the U.S. and the importance of the freedom it provides. I know that I am lucky. All of us who live in the U.S. are very lucky. We live in a country that gives us the freedom to express our opinions and pursue our goals.

Many people will never have the freedom that our country provides. Americans can pursue a dream and create a revolutionary technology, medical treatment, or work of art that changes the future. We can support social, political, or grassroots causes. And we are free to communicate our ideas and opinions. We know that *Life, Liberty, and the Pursuit of Happiness* inspires and distinguishes America.

People who live in many other countries cannot challenge the ideas, policies, or laws of the government. They must follow the plan, career path, and instructions that the government has determined will benefit the country overall. They know that disobedience could affect not only their own life but the freedom and safety of their family.

It is easy to take for granted what we have. It is easy to focus on ideas, people, or systems that need improvement. And the easiest thing to do is to say, "It's not fair," and do nothing. But the easy road could lead to a change in freedom and opportunity.

My mother's family never imagined that the occupation by Japan was possible. Top row, Left to Right: Jose Rosales III (Uncle), Jose Jr. (Grandfather), Remedios (Mother). Bottom row: Evarista Zaraspe (Great Grandmother), Remedios (Grandmother).

I know that this seems impossible.

America could *never* lose power.

We could *never* lose our freedom.

I suspect that the Filipinos thought the same way in 1940.

Only the best

I am committed to providing the best technology, plans, and solutions for the two million men and women in the Armed Forces who serve in 160 countries. They are heroes who act as though the struggle depends on them alone. They act as though their weakness, however small, would reflect on the whole nation. They protect our freedom from those who would take it from us, just as Imperial Japan took freedom from so many during World War II.

Today, global competitor aggression continues to increase. Without a strong National Security, our opportunities and freedom could be lost to us forever.

Military service members, homeland security professionals, and diplomats need the best technology, optimal strategies, and streamlined operations. They are highly skilled, have in-depth experience, and have a strong sense of duty.

National Security leaders at all levels face *Mission Impossible* every day. They must make decisions at the speed necessary for both combat and competition timelines. Strategic, technological, and operational solutions must prioritize opportunities, minimize risk, and anticipate change. *Mission Success* (a phrase signifying the successful completion of all objectives within the required timeframe) is essential.

I know that immediate action to identify technology and resolve shortfalls protects the population during a crisis like COVID. And if a solution neutralizes the efforts of adversaries to seize or control innovation, U.S. economic advantage can be sustained. The work is hard and essential because the National Security business is surrounded by secrecy, threat, and risk. Success is most often signified by *Nothing Happened.*

Today is the day to STEP-UP

Was yesterday just like the day before? The day was calm, and tasks were straightforward. Today will probably be the same, and tomorrow will probably bring few surprises.

Something is missing. Can you remember the last time you were inspired? . . . excited? . . . proud? If you miss that hunger that pulls you to eagerly seek new ideas and answers, or confidently take a chance, ask yourself:

- Do I have a pattern of enduring situations for too long?

- What would make me shake things up?

- What changes could make a difference?

Today, you can step up to an important goal. Important goals, like overcoming the challenges we face as a nation, need the combined talent, singular focus, and commitment of a team.

Like any team that expects to win a Super Bowl, World Cup, or Olympic gold medal, each member of the team has a specific role. Success depends on each person's decision to put the team and goal first. This is easy to say, and much more difficult to do.

Each member of the team puts the team and the goal first by focusing their efforts on the success of others. They must believe that their teammates are loyal, hardworking, and driven to be successful. They must support a team member who is struggling. And they must commit their efforts to compensate for the limitations, oversights, and mistakes of others. There is no place for arrogance or self-interest. Instead, exhilaration and satisfaction are gained in the team's performance and achieving the goal.

Team success also relies on the initiative and innovation that create the competitive edge. Differing experiences are shared within the team which strengthens accountability and accelerates decision-making. With each challenge and success, the team improves. Each member of the team benefits from the opportunity to gain insight from colleagues, learn from mistakes, and avoid future errors.

You have the power to achieve that goal that appears out-of-reach. The impact you can make is in your hands. And when you decide to change your life, things will start to change. Today you can make active decisions to push beyond your current limits.

You already have skills. You want to make a difference, and you are driven to be successful. You can summon the confidence to face the challenges. You can leverage your resources to persevere through adversity. And you can advance through obstacles until you reach your goal. Your life will be more enjoyable and fulfilling. You will find new energy, optimism, and enthusiasm. And you won't have to struggle to invest your time and make progress.

Today you can focus your talent, energy, and commitment on *Mission Success*. And you can create a bigger, bolder, and better future.

The Gemini Way gives you the power to succeed. It instills the optimism to set bold goals. And it brings the focus, energy, and tools to drive forward as a team.

I will introduce you to a mindset that will help you find and strengthen the power that you already have. You will learn how to employ Gemini's unique mindset and to maximize each element of the *Cycle of Success*. And you will see

Mission Impossible?

how to harness external power to accelerate your progress.

Your own *Mission Impossible* can become *Mission Success*.

CHAPTER 2

Impossible Is an Opinion

When was the last time you were *a badass*?

You were inspired, busy, and your energy seemed limitless. Every challenge was an adventure, and the excitement of each step toward success pushed you to action. Success came often. And sometimes, you felt that you couldn't fail. There was no time to think about what might be impossible because you were chasing what was possible and enjoying the adventure.

Impossible . . . Fact or Fiction?

Impossible. How many times have we heard *that*? Is it impossible? Or does it give us an excuse so that we don't have to try?

Many goals were impossible until someone did it. The four-minute mile was impossible until 1954 when Roger Bannister did it in 3 minutes, 59 seconds. In 1903, the Wright brothers made powered, sustained, and controlled airplane flight possible. And Guinness World Records maintains more than 53,000 records. That's 53,000 things that became . . . possible.

Impossible. Maybe some expert said so. Are we sure that they are right? Are we sure that they are an *expert*? And if they are an expert, are their assumptions, data, and logic correct?

If you think that finding the answers to these questions will take a great amount of work . . . YOU BET. So, when someone says *Impossible*, maybe they are saying, "It's not worth my time."

Each member of the Gemini team contributes to keeping the U.S. the global leader by sustaining the premier National Security capability and protecting technical superiority. They faced challenges that many people thought were overwhelming. And they stepped up when others were afraid to try and fail.

In the end, they turned *Mission Impossible* to *Mission Success*—again . . . and again . . . and again.

September 11 is a day that changed the world.

To support Operation Enduring Freedom (OEF) in Afghanistan, Gemini implemented a program to accelerate the delivery of critical equipment and materials to Special Operations Forces worldwide.

The program used local resources to expedite the replacement and repair of equipment . . . and reduced delivery from six months to two weeks. Our efforts significantly contributed to U.S. military success against the Taliban and Al Qaeda.

To fight the improvised explosive device (IED) threat to military forces overseas and prevent homegrown terrorist attacks, a Gemini intelligence team completed 24,000 intelligence tasks—4,000 mission products and actions, 6,300 support requests, more than 13,000 evaluations, and almost 700 reports. Their work halted terrorist activities and prevented IED attacks. Their products helped law enforcement and homeland security agencies identify and capture the Boston Marathon bombing suspects, and supported France after the 2015 terrorist attack.

And in 2019, a customer sent a Gemini team across the country to investigate supply chain issues vital to U.S. strategic nuclear defense capabilities. Our investigation uncovered defects in a $5 electrical component. We implemented corrective action within the authorities of the Defense Production Act Title I, which required acceptance and priority performance of contracts and allocated materials, services, and facilities to promote national defense. According to Congressional testimony by a National Nuclear Security Administration official, our team's actions prevented an eighteen- to twenty-four-month delay in the program and saved U.S. taxpayers more than $1 billion.

The members of the Gemini team are different. They know that their solutions advance vital security interests and keep us safe. They know that our National Security leaders and the men and women who serve the country count on them.

At Gemini, failure is not an option. *Mission Success* CANNOT be impossible. *Mission Success* may not have been achieved yet, but it definitely will. *Mission Impossible* is not fact or fiction, it's just an opinion!

Success begins with me

I believe that leadership is a gift that my team gives to me; my job is to deserve it. Each day I work to serve my team *The Gemini Way*.

Having the best team starts with being the best leader. The best leaders never let their people down. I know that each member of my team wants to be successful and wants to make a difference. My job is to lead them to success. I must be All-In on every challenge, for each member of my team and for every customer . . . every day.

Winning is not easy. Beating the odds is not easy. As the CEO of Gemini, I set the standard for the company. I give to each member of the team the respect, loyalty, and commitment that I want them to give to their customers and to each other. I don't ask a member of my team to work harder than I work for them. And I complete the actions that help them succeed.

I must be a fierce competitor to other firms, both large and small. I must prioritize the needs of my team and customers. And I must hold myself to a *No-Fail, No-Excuses* performance standard.

My customers are principled and devoted to the country. They are winners. I am successful when my team achieves their goals, and the customer can declare *Mission Success*. I aggressively push myself forward, making sure that I live the values of Gemini.

I know that the Gemini team will come up with the solutions no matter how big the challenge, or how short the time. I know this because they are a unique group of individuals who have extraordinary talent, drive, and a genuine loyalty to each other, to the customer, and to the country.

Gemini's success depends on my ability to leverage resources, to motivate progress, to achieve goals, and to strive for more—year-after-year. Whether I am advancing Gemini's business growth, improving operations, or supporting project execution, I think BIG and take a rigorous approach to pursuing goals.

I look at the opportunities and risks for the coming month, quarter, year, and five years. I look at our performance against the metrics and standards that we have set. And I determine the changes that we should make to improve.

For me, success is a WOW. If you are asked to complete a task and you deliver on-time, you are capable and responsible. If you do more than what is expected by resolving other important issues while still completing your task on time, people will say (or think) . . . WOW.

So, if my team says WOW, it's a success. If my customer says WOW, it's a success. And if they both say WOW . . . it's time to raise the standards . . . up the stakes . . . and shoot for more tomorrow.

All of this is easy to say. These words are easy to write. Doing it . . . is different. Gemini's customers and project teams are located at more than twenty locations across the country. The work ranges from physical and information security to budget analysis, manpower planning and advanced research, to Joint Staff planning and high-level expertise.

My workday starts at 5 a.m. I work with members of my leadership team on meeting immediate priorities and the needs of staff and customers. We discuss status and next steps. And we weigh the risks and return on investment associated with new ideas. I also meet periodically with customers and staff members to discuss Gemini's performance, priorities, and issues, and to get their feedback on ideas and future changes. And I support other leaders through my Harvard CEO Group and programs for the Bush School of Government and Public Service and the Matt Light Foundation.

The days are shorter on weekends . . . 5 a.m. to 3 p.m. These days are dedicated to Gemini's goals. I review progress on the goals for the current quarter and make any changes needed to make sure that we meet our goals for the year. I also look closely at the goals for the month. Based on our progress to date, I determine the tasks that we must complete during the week ahead, and the actions, individuals, and products that are essential to success.

This work is essential to success. I do it because Gemini's success is my responsibility. I am not suggesting that anyone should put in the hours that I work. I do it because *Mission Success* saves lives.

Success is the only acceptable result.

A Typical Day

0500 *- 0800*	• *Read about current events, trends, and innovations.*
	• *Review income from sales and investments for Gemini, the Stock Program, and new ventures to identify opportunities, risks, and next steps.*
	• *Review the status of priorities of the week, and determine changes in resources, actions, and assignments.*
0900 *- 1130*	• *Meet with Directors, Project Managers, and Teams to discuss priorities and milestones.*
1200	• *Lunch meetings.*
1330 *- 1500*	• *Discuss performance, progress, and priorities with customers and obtain feedback.*
	• *Assist business associates and community partners.*
1530 *- 1545*	• *Look at stock market indicators and take appropriate buy/sell actions.*
1600 *- 1730*	• *Review status of new business ventures and update priorities, actions, and milestones.*
	• *Provide updates to leaders & staff.*
	• *Research new ideas.*
1800 *- 2100*	• *Attend CEO, Business Council, and Non-Profit Board meetings and events*
	• *Take training courses.*

From unmanned systems to apprehending terrorists

National Security leaders must select the optimal combination of strategies, technology, personnel, and logistics to counter threats and to further the interests of the U.S. The issues are complex, and the factors are numerous.

Gemini experts analyze information across a wide range of areas, assess trade-offs, and propose solutions for consideration and execution by leaders within Defense, Homeland Security, and other federal agencies.

Gemini has contributed to the development of Unmanned Aerial Systems, Special Operations Forces (SOF) plans, and efforts to apprehend terrorists. Project teams work on some of the most important projects around the globe. Some are in the news. Others, you will never know about, because innovative solutions and rapid response addressed the threat and secured the future of America's National Security.

Gemini provides strategic and technical support, clear and disciplined thinking for National Security challenges, and top-tier talent.

Gemini specializes in complex, high-priority challenges . . . applying an All-In approach and a *No-Fail, No-Excuses* performance standard to ensure that each customer is a *Winner*.

Project teams perform tasks in a range of areas, including program execution, advanced technology, intelligence, planning, and operations. They deliver tools to help U.S. forces apprehend terrorists. And they review foreign investment that threatens critical technology, U.S. firms, and our industrial base.

Gemini began operations in 1986 during the rise of the microcomputer, cell phone, world wide web, and cable networks. Projects involved the integration of information technology into facility operations and administrative support. Gemini developed and managed suspense tracking systems for Missile Warning and Space Defense programs. We incorporated bar-coding and supply management tools into Air Force and the Department of Transportation logistics. And we streamlined warehouse, supply, library, mailroom, photography, and graphics operations.

In the 1990s, Gemini expanded to engineering support and advanced research in areas such as unmanned aerial systems, wireless and mobile system standards, and multimedia data compression. We contributed to major defense systems like the Airborne Warning and Control System, Joint Surveillance Target Attack Radar System, North Warning System, Space Defense Operations Center, and Military Satellite Communications.

Customers rated our performance as *Exceptional.* And Gemini operations expanded to Florida, Virginia, North Carolina, Colorado, Texas, and Nevada.

New projects supported Force Protection programs, Intelligence Surveillance and Reconnaissance, and Aircraft and Navy Combatant Craft systems. And we supported a range of areas, including intelligence, planning and operations, improvised threat defeat, and strategic planning, engagement, and operations. By 2010, Gemini had a track record of success supporting Air Force, Army, Navy, and Special Operations Forces customers.

*Advanced Concept Technology
Demonstration of a system to activate
pain sensors without causing damage to
human organs (2000).*

Our support to Homeland Security began in 2005 with exercise support and policy development. We expanded to systems integration, support to covert surveillance, Coast Guard planning, engineering and environmental support, and Program Management support to Law Enforcement Information Sharing.

Gemini's solutions and performance led to Special Congressional Recognition from the U.S. House of Representatives and Citations from Massachusetts, Virginia, and Florida. We are listed in *Fortune's* Best Places to Work in Consulting and Professional Services. We earned International Organization for Standardization certification. And we won many awards including the Most Innovative Company of the Year, Blue Chip Enterprise, Small Business of the Year, and Blue Ribbon Small Business.

I have faced many challenges in thirty-five years: establishing credibility; competing with established companies, such as L3 Communications, Booz Allen and Hamilton, and Deloitte; and attracting the best and brightest individuals to join the Gemini team.

The greatest challenge came with the Budget Control Act and Defense budget cuts that followed. Budgets were reduced, but mission requirements did not change. Even as mission requirements increased, we would still have to reduce costs by 10 percent, then 20 percent . . . and even 30 percent. Layoffs could mean *Mission Failure*. And salary reductions would devastate the members of the team. Each time the budget was reduced, we took bold action. Each time, the *impossible* became *possible*.

I knew that new challenges would emerge in the years ahead. I also knew that we would keep fighting until customer *Mission Success* was achieved and emerge better than before.

You can do the *Impossible*

You don't have to work in National Security to do the *Impossible*. You don't have to have a college degree or a big bank account. Everyone can succeed. The *Impossible* does not have to serve a greater good. It only has to be important . . . to you.

Success is no accident

The members of the Gemini team are heroes. They are problem solvers. They push themselves and they push each other every day to anticipate opportunities and issues, to suggest creative ideas, and to quickly respond to priorities. They get no credit, fanfare, or applause. They are *The Force behind The Force.*

They know what it takes to deliver great results, and they know that they stand for something that is bigger and better than any single individual's contribution. Their strength comes from knowing that they can succeed.

We encounter many skeptics, detractors, and challengers who ask, "Why bother?" or say, "That's someone else's problem" or "It will never happen." This does not discourage our progress.

Instead, they strengthen our commitment. Each time someone says *Impossible*, we get to work and create innovations. It's only a matter of time until we get it done.

Gemini's success was confirmed again . . . and again . . . and again.

Gemini teams succeed because each member of the team knows that what they do every day is important. They know that the stakes are high and there is no room for even minor errors. These are life-and-death risks. And every time, they step up to conquer *Mission Impossible*.

Gemini teams know that *Impossible* is not a fact. They take pride in *beating the odds*. Many of our staff know that they can because they have done it before. They know that the power of the team will lead them to success. After all, *Impossible* is nothing more than an opinion.

Success does not happen by accident. Success requires hard work and the recognition that the difference between *Mission Success* and "ALMOST" often comes down to inches. And you overcome the biggest obstacles, you *beat the odds*, and you get *Mission Success* by inches.

Today, threats come from every direction. Gemini teams must deal with challenges that they have not faced before . . . and threats that they have not seen before. When they hit a wall, they go over it . . . around it . . . or through it. No matter how tough the road, or how insurmountable the obstacle, they push through.

Gemini's culture stresses the importance of thinking and acting like a *Winner*. Each member of the team knows this and expresses it through their work and interactions. They do what is required to make customers and team members winners. They set very high standards—and meet them.

They demand from themselves: hard work, exceptional performance, integrity, discipline, and loyalty to customers. And they value accountability and fix problems they face. They look past the problem. They determine each element that would exist if the impossible were possible, and if *Mission Success* were already achieved. They define the path to achieve each element, and they don't accept excuses. Instead, they drive forward and make each element a reality.

It is how they deliver WOW . . . to customers, to the men and women who serve the Nation, and to our National Security.

You have the power

You have the power to push past your limits and conquer anything that is important. Motivate yourself to start taking on challenges. The change you seek starts with you.

Today is the day for you to achieve that long-awaited goal. Accomplishing a goal makes you feel powerful and proud. Setting huge goals can be the pedal that pushes you harder. The harder it is to accomplish, the better you will feel when you get it done.

Energy, optimism, and enthusiasm will help you through the challenges. And you won't have to struggle to invest your time and make progress. Things will not always go smoothly but you'll be able to get yourself back on the right track.

Picture the win. Maybe you already have that big goal in mind. This could be the year that the goal becomes reality. The first step is to picture the win. Imagine you have already achieved the goal. Picture the world in which you GOT IT, and answer the following questions: How, where and with whom do you live, work, and socialize? What are you proud of, motivated to do, and grateful for? What do your family, friends, supervisors, and team members say? Make a list of your answers.

When you Picture the Win,
your goal is within reach . . . and much more.

Your answers create a picture, and the picture makes your goal real. Once you see it, you can take the steps to achieve each item on the list.

When the items on your list are done, the picture is complete—and your goal is accomplished.

Keep score. Who would watch a football game if no one kept score? If it's a big goal, you probably can't accomplish it in a day, a week, or even a month. Progress will be gradual. Set objectives for each quarter and month that move you closer to the goal.

The objectives must be quantifiable. For example, "three interviews for a promotion" is quantifiable. For each objective, create an action plan detailing the steps you must take and the resources you need. Each month list the objectives and action plan steps for the month on a whiteboard or large easel pad and check off each item when complete.

Have the courage to succeed. A big goal is scary. It is easy to look at it and think, "What is the point? I can NEVER get that." If you choose that goal and begin to execute a plan, it will be a very different year.

The excitement of the possibility of your massive, wild goal pushes you to action. You become busy pursuing the goal. And you have no time to think about what might have been because you are chasing what is possible and enjoying the adventure. The *impossible* is a by-product of the chase.

It all starts with the courage to do the impossible.

CHAPTER 3

The Power to Succeed

Success requires courage, hard work, and perseverance. Only you can decide to invest your time and resources.

How do people make an investment decision? Do they jump at the first *shiny object* they see? No. It is not a random act. People put work and planning into it. That's why many people will only invest in something based on its performance record and potential for delivering desired results.

My decision to start Gemini in 1986 was rooted in my upbringing. My parents taught me that I could *choose* to overcome any obstacle. As Gemini grew, I realized that Gemini's success is a *choice*. I had to choose to work hard, to learn from mistakes, and to persevere through the frustration and disappointment of competition.

It is this choice that gave me the power to succeed. This choice created *The Gemini Way*, the Aerospace and Defense Company of the Year, *Fortune's* Best Place to Work in Consulting and Professional Services, and a thirty-five-year track record of success.

Learning to succeed

My parents gave me many gifts. They gave me the education, strength, and confidence to do anything.

They were role models and devoted champions. The traditional values they brought from the Philippines, combined with the determination for excellence and American spirit of competition was the foundation of *The Gemini Way*. Gemini's thirty-five-year contribution to National Security is their success as much as mine.

During the years leading up to their U.S. citizenship, my parents worked hard under enormous pressure. To ensure that their immigration status would be renewed each year, they worked hard to give their patients the best care. They volunteered to teach new interns and residents and supported research projects. And they agreed to work on-call many nights and weekends. They worked seven days a week . . . 52 weeks a year.

My parents also worked hard to give their children a good life. They were not *cheerleaders.* They were serious and tough. My parents believed that each of us was talented, strong, and exceptional. And as immigrants, they were determined to arm us with the habits and confidence that no one could ever take away. They had a unique, fierce, and unbounded love for their children.

They faced a challenge that they never expected when I was diagnosed with a rare disorder at age three. *Cone Dystrophy* affects the retina and left me legally blind. There were many appointments with specialists. But there was no cure, no corrective procedure, and no hope that my vision would improve. The decreased central visual clarity, extreme light sensitivity, and inability to see colors would never change.

They told me that there were many things in the world that I could NOT control. They told me that the one thing that I could control was ME. I controlled my choices, my decisions—and my actions.

My parents worked hard to give us a good life. Left to Right: Victoria, Conrado Bondoc (Father), Remedios Bondoc (Mother), Conrado Jr. (Brother), Josefina (Sister) (1963)

To minimize the effects of my disability, I would have to work hard—very hard—to learn. In school I had to develop skills in Math, English, Science, and all the subjects that I would need to be successful in life. I had to earn a master's degree. The master's degree was required, not optional. The degree would help me succeed, no matter what I chose to do in the future.

And they told me that I could overcome any obstacle: all I had to do was choose the goal. "Choose carefully," they said. "Go for the BIG ONES. Don't go for the ones that need *too much run for not much slide*." They were telling me to consider the decision that every baseball player makes to advance to the next base. The runner wants to expend the least amount of energy to slide safely into the next base. The runner wants less run for more slide.

They explained, "Science, Math, and Engineering are structured, straight-forward, and can provide a reliable source of income. Becoming an artist, an actor, or a professional athlete involves more work to compete for fewer jobs. If the pleasure and satisfaction that you would get is so important, OK. Just remember that pleasure and satisfaction won't pay the bills. *Too much run, not enough slide*."

I decided to start Gemini when I was twenty-five. I wanted something *more*. I wanted to do something that made a difference. I wanted something that deserved my best ideas, my best skills, and my best efforts. And I needed something that inspired me.

I knew that building a company would not be easy. I knew that there would be many challenges ahead. But I was prepared to work hard to overcome the obstacles.

I was lucky. My parents had convinced me that I could succeed. And if the worst happened—if opposing forces, Murphy's Law, or bad luck was too powerful, I knew that my parents would be there. I would never be abandoned—or hopeless.

Top performers thrive, and leaders get results

Even a big paycheck has limits. I have seen many talented people who are unhappy in their job. They complete the work assigned and count the minutes to the end of the workday, five days a week, fifty weeks a year.

I decided to create a company where top performers thrive, and National Security leaders get results. I wanted to offer employees advancement, the freedom to pursue innovation, and teamwork. I believe that top performers thrive in this type of environment because of the energy, freedom, and camaraderie it provides.

I chose the name Gemini Industries. As the Latin word for twins, Gemini represents the optimal balance between the customer and the employee that promotes success.

What makes Gemini unique?

National Security leaders are responsible for important programs that affect the lives of many people. The goals of these programs are tough, the schedules are tight, and sometimes unexpected events cause huge changes to short-term goals and available resources. Results can be delayed or inadequate.

I realized that I could best assist my customers with a Gemini focus on **ideas** (instead of objections), **action** (not just promises), and **results** (not excuses). I wanted Gemini to become known for:

- Innovative ideas to solve problems
- Rapid response and proactive support
- Successful delivery of on-time results

If Gemini minimized objections, promises, and excuses, then the progress of customer programs would improve. If Gemini consistently overcame obstacles, then energy, and momentum would compel results. Success could come easier and faster.

I wanted to create a culture of top performers and an integrated team of the best performers in different fields. If I could create a culture that would inspire top performers, my teams would contribute more to customer *Mission Success—* and deliver WOW.

I used my own experience in the workforce as a starting point. I had worked for four years as an engineer supporting Missile Warning systems; Command, Control, Communications, and Intelligence (C3I) systems; and anti-ballistic missile programs. The work was interesting. But I was frustrated. I was frustrated by bureaucracy, company policies, and processes that seemed to promote delay and indecision.

My first job was at a defense engineering firm. I was tasked to prepare a report on the communications supporting missile warning. I was twenty-one years old and very excited. "This is important!" I thought. "I have to get this right. I don't want a missile to get us."

They gave me the resource material, in twenty piles of reports that sat two-feet high on my desk. I worked late every day for two weeks. I read every report. I found each radar, satellite, and circuit. And I created a big table to organize the speed, type, and level of each communications device.

Then the trouble began. The data in the reports didn't match. My supervisor explained why the reports might differ. He pointed out that the reports were prepared during varying timeframes and system upgrades could have changed the device, speed, type, or level. But my supervisor could not tell me the information that was correct. The solution was to create a disclaimer stating that the information in my report may or may not be correct.

I couldn't let it go. There was a right answer and a wrong answer somewhere. Then, an idea came. All the missile warning communications had to go through the Cheyenne Mountain Complex in Colorado Springs, Colorado. The installation supported the North American Aerospace Defense Command (NORAD) aerospace warning and aerospace control missions, and it warned of ballistic missile and air attacks against North America. The information in the Cheyenne Mountain Complex communications center must be complete and accurate.

I called the communications center. An Air Force Sergeant sent to me a computer-generated report that contained the information I needed. I entered the information in my table and my research was complete. I was very proud.

My supervisor was not proud. I had failed. I should not have called NORAD. I should have written a memo to the Project Manager requesting the data from the Cheyenne Mountain. The Project Manager would forward the request to the Colorado Springs office to obtain the data. This process could add weeks to the schedule, but the delay was unimportant.

Over time, I realized that many processes favored talk over action. My project teams would discuss the same issues and options over and over again. Sometimes it seemed that reaching a solution was unimportant. I sat through endless meetings that I can only describe as *Hockey Games*. Ideas were passed around like a hockey puck:

- *Slapshots*—raising a loud objection,

- *Slashing*—mentioning someone's past oversight or objection, and

- *Icing*—taking a break if the discussion became too heated.

But no one ever scored, and the meetings always seemed to end the same way—"Let's get together next week to see where we are."

Gemini had to be unique. It would have to promote innovation, teamwork, and career advancement and minimize tasks that create frustration. It had to inspire top performers to apply their skills to deliver WOW.

On the move to a $10 million business

I had an idea and a company. Now what? I knew nothing about business. The Math and Computer Science courses did not cover any material about running a business. I had never taken a business course. My knowledge was close to zero.

I worked hard to learn each area of business operations and development: accounting, human resources, contracts, security, marketing, sales, and technical operations. Fortunately, the members of my family— the earliest members of the Gemini team—were 100 percent behind me and 0 percent paid.

My brother and sister gave me books on entrepreneurship and a wide range of business topics. I studied each area to understand the tasks to be performed; the people, tools, and capital I would need; and the timing of actions.

I needed sales. I traveled to Washington, DC, every two weeks. I went to Texas in the heat of the summer. I even flew to Cleveland in a snowstorm. I wrote proposals for Air Force work. And I presented briefings to NASA.

*The Joint STARS simulation allowed the
Air Force to preview functionality prior to
full development (1999).*

The work paid off. I won five $3 million contracts to support Defense, Transportation, and Health and Human Services. By the end of 2000, Gemini had a $10 million business base, offices in Massachusetts, New York, and Virginia, and a team of extremely talented and dedicated professionals.

Are you ready to go BOLD?

The world is moving faster every day. The days, weeks, and months seem to go by in an instant. How are you doing on your *bucket list*? Did you finish the career, family, or personal goals on your list of New Year's resolutions?

Next year can be an exciting adventure. It can be a year that inspires you . . . when your energy seems limitless. Are you ready to be BOLD?

Success requires significant effort. Winners think BIG and take a rigorous approach to pursuing goals until they succeed—believing all along that they will.

The Gemini Way is the right choice to do the *Impossible*. It is a powerful tool if you are facing an overwhelming challenge and want to be a winner. It harnesses power. It fuses the power of decision, the power of momentum, and the power of perception to reinforce your courage to face crazy odds, to stay motivated through the difficult times, and to succeed.

Things change. The economy, politics, competition, and the threat will all change. Although the quality of information, technology, and tools may change, *The Gemini Way* will not change. Your mindset is essential to your success and *The Gemini Way* is built on a unique mindset that balances fierce competition, teamwork, and duty.

This mindset applies the power of decision to your benefit. There is great power in *decision*. Once you decide on an action, a plan, or a goal, many things lose power over you. Distraction loses power over you. Fear loses power. Procrastination loses power. Suddenly, you can move forward and achieve things you thought were impossible. This happens because you have already made the decision. This mindset gives you courage. The status quo and sacred cows no longer limit you. You want to think out of the box to achieve the objectives and create a better tomorrow.

The Gemini Way also uses a methodology to maximize the four elements of success: potential, action, results, and attitude. The methodology focuses activities and highlights actions that limit progress. It helps you focus efforts, assess your progress, and sustain momentum. I call it—the Big MO.

The Big MO gets you further with less effort. It is the power that makes you feel like you can't lose. You will accomplish much more in less time. And when the Big MO is gone . . . it will be hard to get it back.

The Gemini Way will concentrate the power of decision, momentum, and perception to lead you to your BOLD goal and to the inspiration and satisfaction of an exciting year.

Achieve your goal

On Easter Sunday in 2009, three Navy Sea, Air, and Land (SEAL) snipers rescued Captain Richard Phillips, master of the merchant ship MV *Maersk Alabama*, after four Somali pirates took him hostage. On September 11, passengers fought to gain control of United Airlines Flight 93 and lost their lives to protect the U.S. Capitol.

Do you ever wonder how people face insurmountable obstacles and mortal danger? How did they become the people who could take the actions necessary to achieve the goal?

You can become that person. You can achieve your goals if you choose to invest talent, time, and effort. You can face challenges, fight through the obstacles, and achieve your goal. It is not easy. It is not even tough. It is demanding and time-consuming. And it will not happen overnight.

Invest Talent: You must believe that your talent impacts success. As you enhance your skills and gain new skills, your ability to succeed improves.

During the early years of Gemini operations, work was scarce. To get one contract, I would have to work as a secretary at Hanscom Air Force Base. During the day, I did the typing, the filing, and I got the coffee. At night, I worked to develop technology tools and databases for the office. My tools changed the way Hanscom did business. They were also the platform on which I built Gemini.

Invest Time: You will have to work many hours to get past the obstacles to your goal. You will need three different plans.

Plan A is your most direct route to the goal. It takes advantage of the opportunities to achieve the goal and best positions you for future success. Plans B and C are the plans that you will have to follow if obstacles or unforeseen changes make Plan A impractical.

Each year I set a goal for Gemini's growth. Growth can be achieved by pursuing new customers for current services, adding products and services, or purchasing a viable company. Plans A, B, and C for the year use one or more of these strategies based on the goal and factors such as market volatility, economic feasibility, and risk.

Invest Effort: No matter how hard you work, how carefully you plan, or how talented you are, you will hit obstacles and make mistakes (sometimes . . . big mistakes). You must accept that success is not about getting knocked down.

*"I Have Not Failed. I Have Just Found 10,000
Things That Do Not Work."*

—Thomas Edison

Successful people get up . . . once, twice, as many times as it takes to succeed. Each time you make a mistake or fall short, you must think about what went wrong and try again.

*Gemini was named 2020
Aerospace and Defense Company of the Year
for innovative solutions across
National Security*

Investing your talent, time and energy in *The Gemini Way* is a big decision. How can you be confident that it will work for you?

The Gemini Way:

- Brought an immigrant with a visual handicap to the Massachusetts Institute of Technology Class of 1981 and a master's degree in Computer Science,

- Led a woman working in a male-dominated field through the *glass ceiling* to become CEO of a multimillion-dollar business, and

- Took a 25-year-old female entrepreneur with a life-long disability from longshot to CEO of the Aerospace and Defense Company of the Year.

I know that it will work—because I lived it.

I also know that you are driven to succeed. You are ready for the energy and optimism that helps you through the challenges. You are ready to face the challenges that improve your skills and increase your confidence.

What are you waiting for?

CHAPTER 4

Delivering WOW

Not everyone wants to be *badass*.

Many people are satisfied being *good enough*. They are respectable and content. And the pull toward *good enough* is strong. Successful individuals know that although learning is hard and failing isn't fun, a WOW brings great excitement and fulfillment. Many have commented late in life how surprisingly fast time passes. The clock is ticking. What are you doing?

When a person does what they have agreed to do correctly and on time, they deserve respect and thanks. Delivering WOW involves more. It meets commitments and exceeds expectations to a level that greatly excites and impresses beneficiaries.

There are many ways to exceed expectations for a WOW. You could contribute to the success of an unrelated high-priority area. You could save your customer (or the taxpayer) a significant sum of money that can be used in critical areas. And if your solution is revolutionary, impacts a wide population, or focuses excitement and esteem on your customer and supervisor, you are sure to get a WOW.

Work ten times harder—Aim ten times higher

It was clear to me early on that delivering WOW was the only way that I could level the playing field. My parents told me that I could only be successful if I worked ten times harder and met ethical, educational, and career standards that were ten times higher.

They sat me down one day and said, "Listen . . . You don't look like everybody else. Many people won't like you. You are small. You're a girl. And you're BLIND. Some people will try to cheat you. You have so much going against you. But you can learn what you need to know. You can become strong and independent. You must decide if you are willing to work hard. If you work hard, ten times harder as everyone else, you can get what you want."

Ten times the work gives you an edge: My parents explained that if two equally talented people work the same amount, each has an equal opportunity to get a job, win a race, or achieve a goal. More work will give you the edge over a competitor with equal skills. They said that my success might need ten times the work just to compensate for my handicap, and any racial or gender bias.

Over the years I worked to improve my nonvisual senses and mental skills. My communication and learning rely more on sound than on visual material and facial expression. So, I worked to develop a superior memory and the ability to sense the tone of a person's voice.

Prior to making a presentation, I memorized the details of ten to one hundred slides. I studied the order of each slide in the presentation. I even memorized the placement of information and graphics on each chart. If I pointed to the wrong graphic, I would highlight my handicap. Even worse, I might appear incompetent. Today, I often remember the comments of each person in a conversation for many weeks, months, and sometimes years. I can remember their ideas, assertions, objections, and commitments.

I have also learned clues that indicate when a person's tone is inconsistent with their words. A person's tone of voice tells me a great deal about how they feel about their message. If a person's statements are concise and clear, it is easy to be confident that they will follow through on their plan. If they are tentative, or their assertion includes many qualifiers or uncertainties, then they may be seeking assistance, or lack the will to follow through.

The skills that I have developed improve my ability to develop plans, support stakeholders and the members of my team, and see weaknesses in my competitors.

Ten times the standard raises performance: Each person works to achieve their own standard of performance. As you raise the standard and move closer to perfection, you will have to invest more time and work to meet your standard. Repetition, analysis, and adjustment improves skills, accelerates execution, generates momentum, and contributes to success.

From age four through high school graduation, my parents expected me to take piano lessons. They knew that learning a piece of music requires hard work, discipline, and concentration. They knew that integrating the right-hand and left-hand parts was impossible without perseverance and hours of practice. And they wanted me to experience the unique feeling of accomplishment and pride that goes with finally mastering a piece of music.

Because of my vision, I had to memorize each Sonata, Waltz, and Etude. I memorized each note, chord, instruction, and annotation in the eighty-page sheet music to play the Beethoven Piano Concerto #1.

Success came with repetition and hours of practice. Eventually my hands learned which notes and chords follow, and I was able to play the music on *autopilot*. The same is true with the strategies, tactics, and tasks in business.

Mastering the Beethoven Concerto (No. 1 in C major, Op. 15) came with memorization, repetition, and hours of practice.

My mother taught me to play chess. She taught me the different moves of each chess piece. She explained how certain pieces such as the Queen, Bishop and Castle could cross the board in a single move. And she explained how to position chess pieces to protect each other.

I learned the game by playing against my mother. In our early games, she would play without a Queen, Bishop, and Knight so that my loss would not occur too early. As my skills improved, her handicap was reduced.

Playing chess taught me to think ahead. I learned to create a plan to achieve a goal—to checkmate the King. And I learned how to position resources to protect each other. Playing chess, I began to instinctively anticipate the moves of my opponent. And I learned to weigh trade-offs to make progress and accomplish a goal.

I also invested a great deal of time researching successful people. Many books, movies, and television shows detail the lives of famous people and their success in business, entertainment, sports, or government. The actions that made them successful could work for me. Why not?

I took the set of actions that led a person to a successful outcome, and I applied it to my goal. Then, I monitored progress each week to determine adjustments needed to correct assumptions and accelerate progress.

Taking higher ground

The foundation of Gemini solutions is—Doing what we are paid to do is not enough. How can we get to WOW?

In *The Art of War*, Sun Tzu advises military leaders to take high ground. Holding the high ground offers an elevated vantage point with a wide field of view and enables surveillance of the surrounding landscape, in contrast to valleys which offer a limited field of view. WOW was the high ground for Gemini.

From the moment I decided to work on Defense projects, I knew that WOW was my only choice.

Two million men and women put on a uniform every day to defend our country. Many leave their family for long periods and risk their lives at hostile locations. I could not sit in the comfort and safety of my office, put in my time, and stop at *good enough*. The soldier, pilot, and Navy SEAL deserved more. They *all* deserve much more.

We have devoted a significant amount of time and effort setting up Gemini policies, processes, systems, and training to improve the products and services we deliver to customers and to improve day-to-day company operations.

International Organization for Standardization (ISO) Certified Quality System: Gemini's vision is to be the *Standard to which all Others Strive*. To achieve and maintain quality, we set up a Quality Management System integrated across all divisions and functions.

We established objectives, monitoring, controls, and procedures and gained employee commitment. Our system was certified by the ISO in 2010 and has passed subsequent biannual recertification audits. The ISO is an independent, nongovernmental international organization composed of representatives from various national standards organizations.

***Great Place to Work®* Certification:** Gemini values each member of the team. To best serve the differing perspectives of individuals, Gemini must provide a high-trust work experience for all.

We commissioned the *Great Place to Work Institute®* to conduct a survey to gain insight on company strengths and identify areas needing attention. Gemini was certified within a week of survey completion. The *Great Place to Work®* is the global authority on workplace culture that helps organizations produce better business results.

Will the customer say WOW?

Mission Success is first and foremost the direct result of the customer's leadership.

At the start of a project, the Gemini Project Manager meets with their customer to discuss the task, product, and schedule requirements. Staff members are assigned to the project based on skills and experience. Facilities, equipment, and materials are acquired. And any administrative, security, and logistics processes are completed. As these activities proceed, the

Project Manager works with members of the Gemini leadership team to plan the WOW. Our rigorous adherence to this process has distinguished Gemini and promoted success for more than thirty years.

Delivering WOW in the Stock Room and the Mail Room: Providing solutions to support high-priority National Security programs does not just happen. Many of Gemini's early projects involved administrative support to facility operation.

- We streamlined procedures, incorporated information technology tools into facility operation, and reduced the cost of operation for our customers.

- We introduced barcoding into the stock rooms and warehouses.

- We used Microsoft tools to track, update, and distribute publications.

- We developed new procedures and introduced cordless telephones to streamline mailroom operation.

We established a solid track record of performance and received numerous awards from customers.

*The Gemini Department of Transportation
Logistics Team streamlined procedures
and incorporated technology into
facility operation (1994).*

Delivering WOW to National Security:
Gemini project teams accelerate program
schedules and reduce customer costs.

On one project, Gemini was tasked to support
the delivery of an urgent capability. We leveraged
in-place capabilities and incorporated advanced
technology to deliver the urgent capability thirty
months early and $30 million under budget.

To support OEF, Gemini's sixty-person team
was assigned in Florida, North Carolina,

Massachusetts, California, the National Capital Region, and worked at international locations such as Afghanistan, Canada, Cuba, Germany, Japan, Qatar, South Korea, Thailand, Turkey, and the United Kingdom. In a year, we delivered more than 4,200 items of tactical equipment, including 2,900 communication devices, 800 field computing devices, 400 mission planning kits, and 120 processing suites and stations to globally deployed SOF.

Gemini financial managers plan, track, and execute the funds needed to execute $10 million to $500 million programs. Some programs involve funding from over one hundred different sources. Gemini analysts closely monitor obligations and expenditures and perform in-depth analyses to ensure that military teams have the technology, equipment, and supplies to execute their mission.

Delivering WOW to the Gemini team

Delivering WOW is not limited to customers. It extends throughout the company.

Individuals who support day-to-day company operations such as marketing, sales, and communications do not settle for mediocre results. They are committed to exceptional performance as they work with counterparts within customer agencies and serve Gemini staff members supporting customer projects.

I have heard many CEOs describe Human Resources as *those people who tell you what you can't do*. Not at Gemini. At Gemini, Human Resources professionals focus on *how to provide the best* for each individual within legal and practical constraints.

They know that each staff member is their *customer*, and the objective to solve the problems that prevent staff members from delivering WOW.

Each year, Human Resources reviews employee programs and seeks opportunities for improvement. In the most recent *Great Place to Work*® survey, staff members rated Gemini in a range of categories, including Competence, Engagement, Equity, Innovation, Justice, Leadership, Respect, and Support. Gemini earned a 93 percent score—higher than the Fortune Magazine benchmarks for the *Fortune*

Top 100 Best Places to Work lists in 2018, 2019, and 2020.

To minimize employee benefit costs, Gemini also conducts an annual competition to select the best-value Medical, Dental, Vision, Disability, and Life Insurance coverage. This process sustains coverage and prevents sharp increases in premium costs.

Members of the Gemini business operations team are the unsung heroes of the organization. The regulations are varied and restrictive. Their work requires meticulous attention to detail. And any delay could ripple throughout the company.

The finance and accounting team makes sure that paychecks, bill payments, and invoices are accurate and on time. They also make sure that funds are available to grow capital for investment income and expansion.

The security team minimizes the wait time to access project information. They develop close working relationships with counterparts within Government security agencies and continually streamline processes. They also administer training in cyber security awareness, operations security, and insider threat and keep staff members informed of security threats.

The individuals who work in Business Development are like a *Super Bowl* team. They pursue fifteen to twenty-five new contracts each year. They work long hours to carefully plan and present each proposal. They highlight discriminators, substantiate assertions, and provide strong references. And they research the strengths and weaknesses of our competitors. Winning a new contract is hard. They often work late nights to perfect Gemini proposals. They know that a new project provides new opportunities for growth for members of the Gemini team—and the win could net $20 million to $350 million in new business.

Promoting *Gemini Family* Values: Many individuals refer to the Gemini team as *The Gemini Family*. This is one of the greatest compliments they could pay to me.

In the Philippines, the family is revered. Filipino family responsibilities are very different from those in many American families (or workplaces).

My grandmother was always a member of my family. She chose to come to the United States in 1960 and lived with us for the remainder of her life. My mother's father and father's parents had passed prior to 1950. I think that they would have emigrated to America with the family given the opportunity.

Growing up, the members of my family actively supported the opportunities and contributed to solving the problems of family members.

When my mother or father were considering a change in job or home, the family discussed each person's concerns. They accommodated our perspective in their final decision. In the same way, we consider the impact of changes to Gemini policies, systems, and operations on staff members and adjust our plans as appropriate.

One Christmas Eve, I received a telephone call. The twelve-year old daughter of a staff member was found dead from an undiagnosed heart condition. The hospital would not release her body without payment. And the insurance company would not release the funds needed without access to the body. Gemini paid the hospital. And the family began the difficult process of funeral and burial arrangements.

Another individual accepted a position and relocated to Texas to support the Gemini project. When they arrived in Texas, they did not yet have a place to live. The Gemini Project Manager invited the new staff member to live with his family until she could secure a local residence.

Sharing the financial benefit of success: The members of the Gemini team have always been integral to company success.

Initially, we recognized staff member performance with bonuses and awards. In 2002, I created a Profit-Sharing Plan to share success with staff members at all levels of the organization. I have transitioned from the Profit-Sharing Plan to a Stock Program to increase the financial share to Gemini employees.

To recognize the contribution of staff members, we set a profit-sharing percentage each quarter after reviewing the profit for that quarter. Quarterly contributions to staff members were determined by applying the profit-sharing percentage for the quarter to employee gross wages for that quarter. Profit-sharing was distributed by wire transfer to each staff member's account.

In 2019, I set up a Gemini Stock Program to confirm my commitment to all members of the team. The program distributes the benefits of capital ownership to employees.

The share value for each Gemini staff member increases as the value of Gemini stock increases. As their performance improves, stock value increases. As Gemini's base expands and profit increases, the value of the Stock Program grows. And when staff members leave, the members of the Gemini team receive unvested shares of the departing staff member.

Show me the money!—The Gemini Stock Program distributes the benefits of capital ownership to all members of the team (2020).

The ideas, networks, and contributions of Gemini staff members will improve both the projects we perform for customers, and Gemini operations. They will create Gemini's legacy of commitment to National Security that will continue for twenty . . . fifty . . . and perhaps more than one hundred years.

We don't deliver WOW for money, awards, or accolades. Gemini teams deliver WOW because the men and women who defend our National Security deserve WOW. We deliver WOW because that is what the members of the Gemini team deserve.

Gemini delivers WOW because that is who we are.

CHAPTER 5

The Power of Decision

Ray Kroc made McDonald's the most successful fast-food corporation in the world. He joined McDonald's in 1954, after the McDonald brothers had franchised six locations and set the stage for national expansion. He grew up and spent most of his life in Oak Park, Illinois. During World War I, he lied about his age to become a Red Cross ambulance driver at age fifteen. During the Great Depression, he sold paper cups and played the piano in bands.

Michael Jordan became a global cultural icon after leading the Chicago Bulls to six national championships and popularizing the NBA around the world in the 1980s and 1990s. He was the son of a bank employee, Deloris Jordan, and an equipment supervisor, James R. Jordan Senior. He tried out for the high school varsity basketball team during his sophomore year, but at 5'11" he was deemed too short to play at that level.

Corazon Aquino served as the 11th President of the Republic of the Philippines and was the first woman to hold that office. A self-proclaimed *plain housewife*, she was married to Senator Benigno Aquino Jr., a staunch critic of President Ferdinand Marcos. She emerged as the leader of the opposition to President Marcos after her husband was assassinated upon returning to the Philippines from exile in the United States.

Many ordinary people become champions while geniuses or brilliant individuals never do. Talent, skills, and resources are important. Work, discipline, and determination strengthen skills and expand resources. And mindset brings these elements together.

The Gemini Way gives you the mindset that is essential to success. This mindset gives you the courage to challenge conventional wisdom. And it integrates the characteristics and attitude of a *Winner* with fierce competition, teamwork, and duty.

*I first met Senator Benigno and
Corazon Aquino when my father was
Senator Aquino's doctor in the U.S. (1989).*

The *Winner's* mindset

A *Winner* needs to be extraordinary. Winners
confront conventional wisdom and believe that
both adversity and failure are integral to success.

A winner considers solutions and near-perfect
ideas that can be applied to overcome challenges.
They are very strong and do not take *no* for an
answer. Instead, they look to tackle any situation
that presents itself as a challenge.

Their mindset looks past current circumstances to plan for future success. When things are going well, the mindset takes you higher. It positions you to take advantage of opportunities. The COVID-19 pandemic swept through the world leaving damage in its wake. As people search for motivation, the winner's mindset turns the situation into something positive and seeks opportunities for personal and professional growth.

Winners cannot settle for the ordinary. They must stand out and show the world how good they are. Many challenges arise from adherence to conventional practices that are irrelevant or obsolete. A winner has the courage and motivation to change the norm and understands that adversity is integral to success. Ask every successful person to tell you how many times they had failed at something and you will be amazed. Many of them have pursued opportunities over and over, until the desired result occurred.

You can start to apply this mindset to deal with tough scenarios by identifying the things you are good at, or things that make you happy when you try them out. Focus on those things and ignore the negative. You should also reflect on how the activities around you can be turned to your benefit. The number of opportunities available in the most difficult situations will surprise you.

The Gemini Way incorporates the *Winner's Mindset*. You can achieve anything if you believe in yourself. If you believe in your ability to provide solutions, your efforts will produce results. Although the quality of information, technology, and tools may change, it is your mindset that is essential to success.

Many years after I built Gemini and pursued goals using this mindset, I heard about Emeritus Professor Allan Snyder and his book *What Makes A Champion?*.

Professor Snyder's book explores success and whether or not a *Champion Mindset* can be defined or created. More than fifty champions from a variety of fields (including government, entertainment, sports, business, arts, education, and medicine) are discussed. Professor Snyder identified three main characteristics shared by champions:

- Absolute need to be extraordinary,

- Courage to confront conventional wisdom, and

- Conviction that adversity—even failure—is integral to success.

In *Make Your Bed: Little Things That Can Change Your Life...and Maybe the World,* Admiral William H. McRaven (US Navy retired), U.S. Navy SEAL, and former commander of Joint Special Operations Command describes ten life lessons derived from his time as a SEAL.

Admiral McRaven emphasizes the importance of perseverance through hardship, challenges, and setbacks that test determination. SEAL candidates who *ring the bell* indicate to the instructors, other candidates, and most importantly to themselves, that they have chosen to quit. Quitting is never the answer because as SEAL instructors state, "You never forget quitting."

It seems that research confirms the mindset of *The Gemini Way.* And our success is not just a coincidence.

9/11 and the Special Forces

On September 11, 2001, nineteen militants associated with the Islamic extremist group al Qaeda hijacked four airplanes and carried out suicide attacks against targets in the United States. Two planes were flown into the twin towers of the World Trade Center in New York City, a third plane hit the Pentagon just outside Washington, DC, and the fourth plane crashed in a field in Pennsylvania. Almost 3,000 people were killed during the 9/11 terrorist attacks.

The terrorist attack and the events of September 11 were a major turning point in Gemini's history and changed the company's direction and growth.

We decided to win the SOF contract: In June 2001, I heard about a contract to support SOF. As I researched the SOF mission, vision, and values, my interest in supporting the Navy SEALs, the Green Berets, and Air Commandos increased. I wanted to bring innovative solutions to these elite teams of intense and highly trained *Quiet Professionals* operating as the most trusted force in America.

Retired military commanders and marketing professionals working in the defense community said that Gemini could not win the contract. "You don't know anything about SOF," they said. They were right. We had never executed the Urgent Deployment Acquisition process. And we had no experience performing tasks in public diplomacy or financial analysis of terrorist networks.

We were not discouraged. We started preparing a proposal to secure the SOF contract. We developed a strategy, set up a schedule, and put together a team. On 9/11 the world changed. The country was in shock and chaos. Some of our customers and even Gemini staff members worked in the Pentagon.

It would have been easy to be distracted by the confusion and fear. But I knew that it was time to step up. Now, Gemini *had* to win. We had to win because we were the best ones for the job.

Gemini could not and would not give up. We decided that we were going to compete for the SOF contract, and we **decided to win**. We worked fourteen-hour days for two months. We detailed our technical approach. We identified sixty-five program specialists, financial analysts, and operations experts for assignment to the contract. And we presented a management plan to deliver a range of skills, anticipate opportunities and risks for customers, and efficiently execute tasks. We completed a 400-page proposal.

Less than one month after the terrorists departed from Boston Logan airport headed to the World Trade Center, we departed the same airport to present our proposal in person in Florida. The $120 million SOF contract was awarded to Gemini less than two months later.

We met the urgent needs of SOF from Day 1 of the contract. SOF have urgent needs. They need advanced technology. They need streamlined execution plans. And they need things fast. Accelerated schedules and minimum response time are the norm.

On the day that the Government called to tell us to start work, they told us that we had three days to have the fifty-five-person project team in place. Members of the project team needed specialized skills in advanced concept technology demonstration, signal intelligence, or nuclear biological chemical defense and high-level security clearances.

Commando Solo conducts broadcasts at night to reduce probability of detection in politically sensitive or hostile territories.

We had **decided** to win long before the Government called. To prepare for project start, we negotiated contingent employment agreements with project staff and created a start-up plan that identified critical milestones.

We created checklists of tasks to be performed during project start-up. And we staged resources (including offices, administrative support, information, and logistics). Because we had **decided** that we would win before submitting our proposal, we had a plan. We executed the plan, adjusting any steps to accommodate unexpected issues. All members of the project team were in place on schedule.

Think like a winner

You can think like a winner. You can learn how to be exceptional. You must develop plans, take actions, and complete objectives in a way that makes you stand out.

Most people are satisfied with being *good enough*. They are satisfied with small wins and hold themselves back from great progress. In contrast, winners are not content with where they are. They always look for opportunities and ways to improve their skills and abilities.

Thinking like a winner starts with dedicating yourself to being exceptional. This is different from a dedication to excellence. In addition to excellence, winners must also be *unique*. They make a conscious decision to do what others shy away from and to be the best at anything they do. Winners have a burning desire to keep pushing and to be as exceptional as they can. Nothing holds them back.

Create the *Best Version*: The first step to thinking like a winner is to become exceptional.

Create a mental image of your *best self.* Identify the skills you must attain. If there is a particular position that you must have, push yourself to embody that image. Your mind is a powerful weapon. Your mind is a tool that you can use to shape your life. The efforts of the most talented or skilled person are wasted if you do not believe in yourself.

Create a confident self-image. When you look at a winner or record-breaker, you see that they are confident in their abilities. You must believe in yourself if you want others to believe in you. You must be confident enough to believe that you can overcome any challenge you face. This is the first step that you must take before you begin to take on a challenge.

Accomplish Big Goals: The best people in their fields set big goals and accomplish them.

Winners prime themselves up for huge success as they go about their daily lives. They start by setting small goals and then link everything up to a bigger goal. As they accomplish the small goals, they build confidence in themselves and can pursue and achieve the bigger goals. The process is long and requires sacrifice. But the results can be huge.

Think of that picture of yourself that you created. Look at yourself today and identify the major differences. What would you need to do to get where you want to be?

Identify these improvements and turn them into goals. Break down each goal to suit your daily schedule and find the path to becoming the *best version* of yourself. This is something that you must do every day to get better. Don't hold back.

As you think big, your actions must follow through. Be ready to invest time and effort. Doing the *impossible* is not easy and only comes from a great deal of effort. The best athletes who win medals or play on championship teams owe their success to hours of behind-the-scenes training. If you dream about the things you want but are unwilling to do the hard work, you will fall short.

Avoid the *Shiny Objects:* Life is not fair. The world is not perfect. And many distractions prevent us from achieving goals. I call these distractions the *shiny objects.*

Everyone who wants to be a winner, think big, or pursue an *impossible* goal faces disappointment along the way. Bad things that are outside of your control happen. Someone may take a dishonest or self-serving action that blocks your progress. And sometimes, your efforts just fall short.

The winner resists the temptation to follow the *shiny object* to fear, self-pity, or despair. They know that there are many people who are worse off. A winner thinks about those remarkable individuals who have bravely faced greater injustice, danger, or death, and gains inspiration from their experience and actions.

A setback can also bring on a shiny object that I call *Who Shot Willie?* A setback often compels victims, competitors, and bureaucracies to engage in a highly emotional process to find and condemn the individual who is responsible for the fatal act. Instead, the winner accepts the need to consistently improve processes and knows that they must improve in order to secure future success.

Winners also fight the temptation to engage in the *blame game* and criticize the shortcomings of others. They know that finding the *guilty* will not change the current circumstances. In fact, the search for the guilty is a distraction that delays progress and wastes time, energy, and emotion.

Hold the Line: A winner does not have the choice to quit. They know that they have personal limits. Their talent, skills, and physical strength may not meet a specific standard. But they will not fail because they quit.

Hold the Line is a military tactic in which a line of troops is expected to prevent an enemy breakthrough in order to maintain the existing position or state of affairs.

Winners perform well under pressure. They hold the line and carry on when the world seems to have turned against them. They have learned to deliver the same level of performance regardless of what they are feeling. They maintain resilience in the face of negative pressure. They keep issues in proper perspective without losing sight of the goal. And they understand that change is the only constant.

Winners have spent years challenging themselves each day in ways that were harder than yesterday. Over time, they developed the ability to stay positive and competitive, and to push past the setbacks. They have learned that they could get through setbacks and emerge stronger by remembering that success is not about them.

Winners focus on what they can control. They prepare for challenges by investing in the resources that will help them meet everyday demands, the occasional crisis, and unexpected twists. When setbacks occur, they mitigate the damage, learn the lessons that will help them in the future, and move on.

Winners focus on the long-term outcome and remain steady in the face of real or potential obstacles. They endure in the face of failure because they see failure as an opportunity to grow and improve, not a reason to back down.

They have learned to stay positive when they encounter negative people. They elevate negative people instead of allowing them to ruin the spirit of accomplishment. And since winners are grateful for what they have, they focus on past accomplishments and future achievements, instead of what someone else has.

As a result, winners keep trying until they get it right. Winners never give up.

The decision to serve

Leaders who have served at the highest levels of Defense, Homeland Security, and State have joined Gemini to continue to tackle complex, make-or-break issues. Many individuals came to Gemini after serving in leadership positions in the military or federal government.

Sal Malgari joined Gemini after serving as the Air Force Program Manager and Technical Director/Chief Engineer for programs such as the Joint Surveillance Target Attack Radar System. He chaired Major Defense Acquisition Program Source Selection Evaluation Boards. And he led numerous Grey Beard Reviews of Air Force programs. Sal has been instrumental in establishing Gemini's track record of success, leading teams in the successful execution of $100 million Programs for the Air Force System Acquisition, SOF support, and IED Defeat.

*Members of my team have served at the
highest levels of the U. S. Government.
Sal Malgari (Left), John Higgins (Top Right),
and Pedro Torres (Bottom Right).*

Pedro Torres created and grew the Advanced Solutions Division from one person to more than $300 million in contracts. During his military career, he served as Commander, as Natural Disasters Emergency Operations officer for the Caribbean, and in Special Assignments, including Khobar Towers recovery efforts and Host Nations Coordination in the Central Command Area of Operations.

John Higgins will lead our growth and success in the decades ahead and create Gemini's twenty-first century. He leads the Command, Control, Communications, Computers, Intelligence, Surveillance, and Reconnaissance (C4ISR) and

Homeland Defense Division with the optimal mix of program management, commercial sales, and military experience that has enhanced performance levels. In just two years, he has pursued more than $475 million in new business to grow the Division and open a new office in the National Capital Region.

Gemini's team of Defense Sector Experts lead commercial and economic analyses of impacts to the Air, Space, Shipbuilding, and Nuclear industrial base. They have extensive experience in the Defense Production Act Title 1, Space Force, ship capability impact on naval warfare, and foreign investment in the U.S.

Although these individuals have already served the country, they **decided** to continue to support National Security as members of the Gemini team. Their talent, skills, and experience add power to the team. And the power of their commitment energizes the team and accelerates progress from the impossible to *Mission Success*.

Thinking like a winner is not easy. Don't even hope. At times, you feel that you are running out of time or are too exhausted to keep driving forward. When this happens, a winner concentrates on results and the impact of success on the future. They know that nothing of great value comes easily. This inspires them to find a way to create more time and push beyond their previous limits.

You already have extraordinary talent, skill, and a passion to succeed. Otherwise, you would not be reading these words.

Strong, talented, and dedicated people think, "I am going to do my best. If I succeed, that's great. If I don't, at least I did my best."

The winner thinks, "I will not quit until I succeed."

Is it time to start thinking like a winner?

CHAPTER 6

No-Fail, No Excuses

There it is . . . that picture of you—a *badass*.

You are already starting to see it. You—confident, witty, thinking fast on your feet, and getting what you want. You're starting to feel it—the swagger, the smile, and the rhythm that goes with power, authority, and dominance.

The Gemini Way employs a unique mindset that balances fierce competition, teamwork, and duty to ensure *Mission Success*. Gemini goes All-In and applies a *No-Fail, No-Excuses* standard to ensure that each customer is a winner.

The *No-Fail, No-Excuses* concept began more than fifty years ago. *No-Fail* is based on my belief that success depends on the decision to achieve a goal (Chapter 3), working ten times harder (Chapter 4), and refusing to give up

(Chapter 5). The *No-Excuses* component came from my limited tolerance for excuses. I cannot remember an excuse that my parents used or accepted.

My parents expected their children to excel ethically, academically, and professionally. Gender and handicap did not affect their high standards. My sister's standards were the same as my brother's standards. She received no consideration in any school subject, including Math, Science, and Physical Education. There was no excuse for a lower grade. And my Cone Dystrophy handicap was not an excuse for less work, diminished performance, or limited results. The standards and expectations applied equally to all.

My parents wanted the best for us. They were not indifferent or uncaring. They were not cruel. Looking back, I think that they were practical and strong. They viewed success and money as a resource that allows you the freedom to make personal decisions and to pursue the goals you choose.

They knew that personal preferences and self-interest would always factor into the choices of people in the world. But my parents also believed that in the end, reason and fairness would prevail. And decisions in educational institutions, companies, and government would be based on quality, results, and merit. So, excuses would prevent us from setting high goals, doing our best, and succeeding.

All-In—Every Day

Gemini is All-In on every challenge, for every customer every day. Each Gemini staff member goes All-In for their team. And the team goes All-In for the customer, *Mission Success*, and National Security.

Gemini's strength lies in a culture rooted in the values of hard work, discipline, and loyalty to the customer.

The Gemini culture stresses the importance of thinking and acting like a *winner*. Gemini staff members know it and express it through their work and interactions. They do what is required to make team members winners. They demand accountability from themselves and from each other, and they fix problems without waiting for outside encouragement. This allows Gemini teams to set very high standards—and meet them,

Drive, accountability, discipline, team-orientation, and focus on improving creates the strong foundation of *The Gemini Way*. The culture also fosters innovation, exceptional performance, and team commitment. Staff members at all levels inspire new ideas and innovation and discourage *go-along to get-along* attitudes.

Discussing innovative National Security solutions with the Under Secretary of the AF and Chief of Staff at the "Futurist Ideas: Forecasting Change" Forum (2015).

We have already discussed how a person can choose to succeed and the power of that decision. The work does not end there. Gemini staff members take a disciplined approach to thinking and acting like a winner and mastering the skills that give them the edge.

The members of the Gemini team push themselves to think and act like winners and to quickly-respond to priorities and needs. This did not happen overnight. Thinking and acting like a winner comes with the investment of time and work to become an ICON.

ICON stands for: Invest in success; Create a "Yes, if" strategy; Open-up; and Never be late.

Invest in Success: Gemini project teams solve problems, seize opportunities, and guide the future of the team.

Each member of the team dedicates their talent, skills, and energy to the goals and success of the team. They know that they are important because there is a direct relationship between their success (or failure) and both team success and customer *Mission Success*.

Create a "Yes, if" Strategy: Gemini teams create strategies to accomplish goals.

Creating a long "No, because" list of obstacles to a strategy is easy; and the list is long. Instead, Gemini teams create a "Yes, if" list. This list is the set of conditions that would have to exist in order to successfully accomplish the goal. As they create the list, they see that many items on the "Yes, if" list can be completed. Then, they complete each item, enlisting stakeholders as appropriate to help.

Each Gemini team member meets periodically with their supervisor to discuss priorities, performance, and any adjustments to accelerate progress on tasks and goals.

Open-Up: Gemini team members are open to new ideas, suggestions, and criticism.

They overcome the urge to say, "I already did that" or "That doesn't work because. . ." Instead, they ask questions such as:

- How will this help me complete a task, or achieve a long-term goal?
- Where has this worked before?

- Do you know anyone who can help me with this?

The answers help them to refine and strengthen their approach and solution.

They know that there will likely be at least ten disappointments for every success, and they learn something from every disappointment. They look closely at each disappointment, and never make excuses.

They list the unexpected events, incorrect assumptions, and mistakes. And they use the list to modify their strategy and try again.

Never be Late: Members of the Gemini team strive to be early, not on time.

Completing tasks two days early allows Gemini teams to meet deadlines when the unexpected occurs. Completing a task early also gives them the opportunity to have a member of their team review the product and catch careless errors. They also arrive at meetings five to ten minutes early. Arriving early affords the opportunity to learn from others.

When a person is late, they are telling the team that they do not care. When tasks are late, the person who has been assigned to complete the action has concluded that the deadline and the person who set the deadline are unimportant. And when a person arrives late to a meeting, they are telling everyone at the meeting that their time and responsibilities have little value.

If you think that becoming an ICON is easy . . . Think again. Like most things worthy of admiration or respect, you must commit yourself to the drive, discipline, and improvement required. Once you do, you will find that momentum builds, and advancement comes more quickly.

An ICON brings drive, energy, and confidence. They inspire others to aggressively pursue opportunities, to solve problems, and to enhance performance. Each day becomes an adventure. And both the successes and disappointments motivate the ICON to take on and accomplish the next challenge.

Bring it on

Gemini project teams apply the *No-Fail, No-Excuses* performance standard that links Gemini success to customer success.

No-Fail, No-Excuses means, "Bring it on . . . We are on it, and we will get it done." Gemini teams know that they can overcome any challenge and succeed if they work together. They know that excuses are a waste of time. They know that excuses distract you from solving a problem. And they know that they succeed . . . when the customer succeeds.

BLUF: In the military, BLUF is an acronym for *Bottom Line Up Front*. On the battlefield, decisions are critical, and time is limited. *Bottom Line Up Front* communicates the critical information needed and a framework to determine next steps.

Members of the Gemini team have learned how to BLUF. Their responses are direct, and they present the key information in the first two sentences.

Each day they are asked for the status of a task, a solution to a problem, or an opinion. When asked, *When will the estimate you are working on be done?* they respond with the approximate percent complete of the task (e.g., 70 percent) and commit to a completion date.

Problem-Solver . . . not Critic: The military commits to *Mission Success*. Problems must be solved. Failure is not an option.

Gemini staff members know that their Gemini supervisor and customer expects them to understand the priorities and complete required products. They bring positive energy and drive to completing tasks and making the team successful.

Some people think that they are contributing when they point out flaws in the ideas of others. Although criticism may get attention, it does not reflect well on the critic. Gemini's customers want to know the risks and how to mitigate them. When Gemini disagrees with a proposed idea or solution, we work to find a better idea or solution for consideration and approval.

Gemini teams maintain a positive outlook through challenges and disappointments. There will always be times when things go wrong, when you don't get what you want, or when your boss chews you out. It is tempting to say to yourself (and to anyone who will listen) "It's not fair!" or "What a jerk!" or "I hate this place." Our customers want to know that Gemini teams learn from mistakes and are always improving.

Gemini teams know that they can overcome any challenge and succeed if they work together (2021).

Gemini staff members demonstrate commitment in actions, not words. When assigned to complete a task by a specified date, they get it done. When they are responsible for products, they ensure that quality, cost, and schedule goals are met. And if a mistake is made, they learn from it and step up to the next challenge.

One Gemini staff member was injured during a mission while serving in the Army. During the past fifteen years, he has undergone numerous surgeries, and has been rushed to the emergency room countless times. The lasting effects of his injury are unpredictable and can cause him to be out for a few days, weeks, or months. Despite his condition, he started a new Gemini Division.

Gemini succeeds because our values-based culture demands drive, accountability, discipline, teamwork, and focus on improving from each individual.

From words . . . to action . . . to *Mission Success*

Saying All-In is not enough. Wanting to be All-In is admirable. Going All-In and being All-In is what makes the difference. All-In is intimidating, demanding, and tough. That is why it powers through, dominates, and delivers.

Being All-In starts with learning the A-B-Cs. Gemini staff members succeed because they have mastered the A-B-Cs of the battlefield. The A-B-Cs give them the edge in solving problems and creating solutions that contribute to *Mission Success*.

I have supported the military for many years. Over the years, I have seen how military leadership, strategies, and tactics make our men and women in uniform the best in the world. Gemini uses these concepts to turn *Mission Impossible* to *Mission Success* and deliver WOW.

On the battlefield, military leadership and training creates a team that will execute the Mission . . . until it's done. The leader must have attention to detail, make big decisions, and have credibility, or the team and *Mission Success* is at risk.

So, the A-B-Cs of the battlefield are:

A. Attention to Detail

B. Big decisions and the courage to make them, and

C. Credibility.

Attention to Detail: The military teaches a person to do the little things right, before trusting them to do the big things right.

The military spends a lot of time on attention to detail. Soldiers make their bed to perfection. Socks are rolled a certain way. And uniforms are inspected from the starch in the hat to the shine of the belt buckle.

Attention to detail is easy to say but very hard to do. It requires extra work. It requires extra time. And it requires discipline. Gemini project teams make a list of reasons that the task assigned is important. They discuss how it will impact the team, customer, Mission, and the future. They create a schedule with milestones for completing the task, which includes at least 3 interim reviews along the way. And they plan to complete the task days early.

Big Decisions: The military trains leaders how to make decisions when they don't have all the information they would like, or when there is no time to ask for help.

Members of the Gemini team make big decisions. They list options and identify the Top 3. If there are more than 3 top options, they have not fully analyzed the risks and trade-offs. Having less than 3 options means that they might have overlooked something. When they think that they have the answer, they do a gut-check to confirm full confidence in the decision.

Credibility: Everyone knows that lying, cheating, and stealing are wrong. Credibility is different. Credibility is about trust, and military leadership is based on trust.

A military leader must create an environment of trust, so that the team will execute the mission in the face of overwhelming uncertainty, exhaustion, or fear.

Each member of the Gemini team remembers what a person tells them, and if that person follows through. When they receive an email asking for something, they do not wait for the second or third email, they get to work. And when they tell someone that they will follow up on something, they follow-up.

*The A-B-Cs of the battlefield give
Gemini the competitive edge (2017).*

Gemini knows that often a person gets only one chance to earn trust.

Gemini project teams push past the limits of their creativity, skill, and stamina to get the best solutions. After the customer makes the decision to select a solution, Gemini executes the actions needed to achieve results. And their unwavering support continues, despite any disagreement or doubt.

Gemini Chief Operating Officer Sal Malgari embodies the All-In commitment. For almost twenty-five years, Sal is always the first to volunteer his support. His integrity, loyalty, and commitment to Gemini, to customers, and to

National Security has not wavered in twenty-five years.

Through the early years of Gemini operations, I kept my handicap secret. I worried that I would appear to be a liability if they knew the secret. I imagined the discussions of the Colonels. "This is an anti-ballistic missile program. She's blind . . . Why her? . . . Isn't Helen Keller available?" I couldn't take the chance, so my handicap stayed a secret.

The secret took its toll in unexpected ways. Sal told me that I was developing a bad reputation in the industry. Business associates thought that I was arrogant and aloof because I consistently ignored them at industry events. They did not know about my handicap and I did not know that they were at the event. I was ignoring them, and I did not know that they were there. We developed a strategy to alert me when associates were in attendance to avoid future misunderstandings.

In 1992, a U.S. Air Force Base decided to convert the Mail Room from Government to company operations. Gemini was awarded the contract. The initial workload was heavy because Gemini had to process the daily mail and a backlog of undelivered mail dating back two years.

On Monday morning, a few weeks after the contract began, a call came from our Team Lead. One Gemini staff member had resigned, and another had injured their back. Sal headed to the Mail Room. Still dressed in his suit and tie, Sal sorted, metered, and forwarded the incoming mail with the team. For the next two weeks, Sal worked in the Mail Room every day to help the team process the daily incoming and outgoing mail and to sort, deliver, and forward the backlog.

Sal's dedication also advanced the expansion of Gemini's business base to Homeland Security. We submitted our $200 million proposal to provide Global War on Terrorism support in 2004. Homeland Security rejected our proposal because it was received after the deadline.

The proposal was late because after ten attempts, we were unable to upload our proposal to the Homeland Security website. Sal challenged the Homeland Security decision, and our proposal was accepted and reviewed when Homeland Security determined that technical issues had affected their website. Gemini was awarded the contract in May 2005.

Sal lives the All-In commitment and the values of drive, accountability and discipline, teamwork, and focus on improvement at Gemini. He played a pivotal role in securing $300 million contracts to support the AF, SOF, Improvised Threat Defeat, and Homeland Security. And he continues to enhance project execution and business operations.

When you are All-In, your actions reflect and even emphasize your words. Your words will inspire people to take actions, and your actions will lead to success.

Beat the odds *The Gemini Way*

With this *No-Fail, No-Excuses* mindset, you can beat the odds and become a winner.

You can summon the courage to beat the odds if you take action to become an ICON, master the A-B-Cs of the battlefield, and clearly and concisely communicate with customers and team members.

Mission Impossible?

As you work to complete tasks, you will encounter issues. List the circumstances, limitations, and stakeholders that prevent success. For each item on the list, describe the actions that would eliminate or reduce their impact. This process guides you to your "Yes, if" strategy and the completion of your task.

Take the bold step to go All-In. Beating the odds requires mental skill and superhuman teamwork. Team success depends on performance at its top level of ability. The team must merge action and awareness and adjust quickly.

You must cease acting like an individual and start operating as a single entity. Expect to lead or be led depending on team progress and planned actions and risks ahead. You will form a strong bond with the members of your team.

You will have a great advantage. You will perform so well that competitors will steer clear of you.

You can beat the odds.

CHAPTER 7

The Power of Momentum

The Big MO—performance-enhancing, contagious—is your *best friend.*

In *The 21 Irrefutable Laws of Leadership* John C. Maxwell describes the effects of momentum. When you have it, the future is bright, and troubles seem unimportant. When it's gone, even the simplest tasks seem impossible, and it's hard to get going because the future seems dark.

The Gemini Way engages resources to motivate progress to goals. It also harnesses the power of momentum to ease struggle, accelerate progress, and deliver results.

The *Cycle of Success*

Gemini Vice President Pedro Torres created the company's Advanced Solutions Division—and grew ASD from one person with an idea to more than $300 million in contracts.

Pedro joined Gemini in 2002 as a Project Manager. Over the next eight years, Pedro led efforts to execute and increase classified advanced technology programs from $5 million to $100 million.

He developed and implemented an innovative process to quickly deliver capabilities. Pedro's Monitor, Align and eXecute process delivered advanced capabilities to meet the urgent needs of military forces worldwide. And his team consistently met accelerated customer schedules and reduced defense program cost.

In 2010, Pedro wanted to expand Gemini's business base within the Intelligence Community, Law Enforcement, and Private Security. He wanted to offer more with better tools. And he wanted to help new customers cope with tight deadlines while reducing operational costs. His vision was to deliver dynamic products and services.

Pedro used the *Cycle of Success* to further ASD's growth and success. The *Cycle of Success* highlights the relationship between mindset and action and outlines opportunities to quickly progress to desired results.

The *Cycle of Success* contains four elements that describe the progression from interest to success: Potential, Actions, Results, and Attitude. Each element in the cycle affects the next element. Success can be achieved by repeating the cycle and continually improving each cycle element until the goal is achieved.

Pursuing a goal begins with the assessment of the *Potential* for success. The review of the resources available and the actions required to achieve the goal determines potential and the decision to proceed. Each *Action* taken yields results (good or bad), and the quality of *Results* affects confidence and attitude. The resulting *Attitude* changes the *Potential* of success and the cycle continues.

The *Cycle of Success* also highlights the power of momentum during challenging and successful times. Using the framework, the power of momentum can be directed to accelerate progress and success.

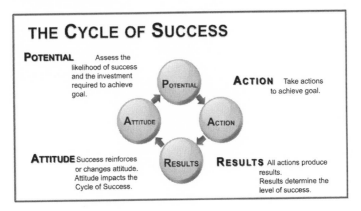

The Cycle of Success outlines opportunities to progress to desired results.

Building a billion-dollar business base

ASD pursued $4 billion and won new contracts supporting Defense agencies, Homeland Security, and Research Laboratories.

Pedro created and grew ASD using two major guidelines:

1. Think BIG. It is you who will set the limit to your success.

2. If you do not *know* that you will succeed, you will not succeed.

He used the *Cycle of Success* to provide advanced technology for the Secret Service, intelligence fusion to support IED defeat, and Air Force advanced research.

Potential: Pedro leveraged Gemini's success supporting SOF to create ASD's business base.

ASD offered services and solutions that were successful in the SOF environment to new customers. As they prepared proposals for a variety of customers, ASD's ability to describe the discriminators of Gemini solutions increased. As ASD won work and delivered WOW, its track record of success increased, and new customers were added. With each win, opportunities increased.

Action: ASD prepared more than one hundred proposals valued at $4 billion.

ASD pursued projects requiring Gemini's core capabilities, new contracts for existing Gemini customers, and products and services outside Gemini's comfort zone.

Many times, the ASD win was unexpected. For example, although ASD was confident that they could effectively support the Walter Reed

National Military Medical Center, Gemini had not previously supported a Medical agency. The investment of time and resources led to ASD's first contract at Walter Reed.

Results: ASD business development results were determined by win rate.

In 2011, ASD won its first multimillion dollar contract to deliver integrated technology solutions to support federal law enforcement agencies.

Over the next five years, ASD began projects to support Joint Programs for Defense agencies. ASD expanded into strategic planning, engagement, intelligence fusion, and international liaison. By its tenth anniversary, ASD had established its expertise to National Security leaders

Gemini uses win rate as a metric to measure the success of business development activities. Each year the win rate is calculated by dividing the dollar value of contracts won by the dollar value of bids submitted.

As ASD increased the number of proposals prepared, the win rate increased. Although winning work for a new customer may be unlikely, Pedro knew that the probability of success is ZERO if the opportunity was not pursued and no proposal submitted.

Attitude: Each win and new contract brought excitement, confidence, satisfaction, and the enthusiasm to pursue new work.

ASD's approach to business development, execution, and growth became more aggressive over time. Pedro took bold actions to identity and win new business. The power of momentum is evident in the win rate that doubled since 2015.

The effect of misfortune and disappointment also takes a toll on the team. In 2016, ASD competed for a contract replacing an ongoing effort. The contract would also increase ASD support. The customer had rated ASD performance *Exceptional* for five consecutive years. Confidence was high.

The team was shocked when the customer excluded ASD from the competition. A company on the ASD team had misrepresented their conflict of interest. In the two years following the loss, ASD's win rate fell by more than 50 percent.

See Incoming?—Return Fire

In the military, *Incoming* is a warning that something (such as enemy fire) is coming toward you. *Return Fire* is doing what is required to protect yourself if you have been fired on, or otherwise attacked.

ASD has faced *incoming* from many directions during the past ten years. Pedro and his leadership team never flinched. They carefully reviewed possible courses of action. And they aggressively executed the steps necessary to eliminate the threat and minimize damage.

During the first year of ASD operations, expenses for items that were delivered to another firm were listed on Gemini bills. A small group of staff members had taken Pedro's idea and formed their own company to compete against ASD. They were spending their workday actively marketing their new company instead of performing ASD tasks. And they had taken ASD networks and funding to build their future.

It seemed that self-interest and greed had emerged, erasing integrity and loyalty. They had betrayed Pedro, ASD, and Gemini. Each staff member involved was questioned. Since their names were listed on the formation and registration documents of their new company, no individual involved denied their actions. All individuals were promptly released.

In 2012, the Budget Control Act and Defense budget cuts threatened ASD. Although mission requirements increased, they would have to reduce costs by 10 percent to 30 percent. It was clear that the budgets would not cover the salaries of the team. ASD needed $1 million—quickly. And we would need $2.5 million more each year to avoid layoffs and salary cuts.

I decided that investing in the stock market was the only way to generate the funds required to meet payroll demands. I structured a portfolio of stocks and mutual funds. And I apportioned the capital into separate professionally managed and internally managed brokerage accounts.

The strategy worked. We generated $2.5 million (on average) each year. The investment income was enough to cover salaries.

Each time events, circumstances, or competitors threatened ASD, we fought aggressively to protect staff members, sustain top performance, and continue to WOW customers

ASD . . . Blueprint and the Future

Do you want to create a service or product that your customer or industry is missing? Do you want to have the opportunity to make the decisions and mistakes to succeed? Do you want to change the world? Starting a new Division could be your future.

You can use the ASD strategy as a blueprint for creating your new Division. You can leverage your enthusiasm, skills, and success to a new service or to bring new customers to Gemini. The services do not have to be revolutionary. The customers can be in National Security, the public sector, or private industry. What is important is that you have a clear vision of your Division and a strong commitment to success.

Today, ten years after the start of ASD, contracts are valued at more than $300 million and operations extend from California, Colorado, Wisconsin, and Maryland, to Massachusetts, Virginia, Ohio, Texas, and Florida. Pedro has strong leaders whose project teams deliver WOW to customers.

Over the years, ASD project teams have delivered complex solutions to support National Security projects.

- **Senior Experts** created solutions to address the high-priority threats.

- **Scientists and Analysts** delivered critical capabilities to support Combatant Commanders.

- **Strategic Planners** developed campaign plans and concepts of operation and supported Joint Staff activities.

- **Architects, Planners, and Engineers** executed design/build projects, provided construction oversight, and supported hazardous waste management and disposal.

ASD's innovative solutions have solved complex problems and received many *Exceptional* ratings and reviews from customers.

*ASD delivers solutions to complex problems
at multiple locations across the U.S.*

"[Our organization] has many short fuse requirements to support the mission and Gemini's team rose to the challenge and provided exceptional support; going above and beyond on a constant basis."

—Secretary of the Air Force

"Gemini's outstanding performance continues to greatly enhance the efficiency and effectiveness of the overall support JIDO provides to the Warfighter and its stakeholders."

—Joint Improvised-Threat Defeat Organization

"The Gemini Tampa team has been extremely helpful, professional, and active from the first day of award to the first day of the contract. At no point over the last weeks were we not on the same page and moving in the same direction."

—U.S. Army

"Based on my 20+ years of service, the team led by Monira is at the top. . . . [The] team is on top of the 100s of actions for each program officer, such that no situations become problems. . . . It has been an honor to work with this team."

—Air Force Research Lab

The strategy employed to plan, build, and operate ASD is a blueprint for success. Perhaps you already have an idea. Maybe you have the desire to create a Division and need help creating or refining your concept. Talk to your supervisor or a member of Gemini's leadership team.

ASD began with a big idea. It was built on a robust foundation fortified by the *Cycle of Success*, and it thrives because of the talent, skill, and energy of the members of the ASD team.

You can have the same success. I know that you can.

As you adopt the All-In approach and the *No-Fail, No-Excuses* standard becomes second nature, your perspective changes, your skills improve, and your resolve strengthens. When combined with a framework that pushes you forward through difficult situations, your power to turn *Mission Impossible* to *Mission Success* will emerge.

The enthusiasm is growing.

The intensity is building.

Ask a question.

CHAPTER 8

Drive for Priorities to *Mission Success*

On the basketball court, Michael Jordan was a *badass*.

He wagged his tongue before a drive, sported a gold chain, trash-talked, and blasted to the hoop for detonating jams.

But when Michael Jordan first tried out for his High School basketball team, he didn't make varsity. In an interview with ESPN, Jordan said, "It was embarrassing not making that team. They posted the roster, and it was there for a long, long time without my name on it. I remember being really mad too, because there was a guy that made it that really wasn't as good as me."

He channeled his embarrassment and anger into motivation:

"Whenever I was working out and got tired and figured I ought to stop, I'd close my eyes and see that list in the locker room without my name on it . . . that usually got me going again."

Becoming better than everyone else comes from many hours of planning, preparation, and work. Until the end of his career, Michael Jordan was the first person to get to the gym and the last one to leave.

Gemini's customers can achieve *Mission Success* because Gemini teams provide rapid response and execute *No-Fail, No-Excuses* processes that have been successful on Defense, Homeland Security and Transportation projects valued at $3 million to $200 million.

No-Fail, No-Excuses Execution

No-Fail, No-Excuses Execution demands accountability and delivers on commitments. It starts with a resource base of top performers, facilities, technology, and tools. The application of metrics, priority-driven plans, and accelerating actions helps our project teams efficiently complete tasks and deliver WOW.

Team of Action: Gemini teams prioritize overcoming challenges and demand accountability. They work closely with customers and use structured processes to deliver WOW to customers.

Our Team of Action uses structured processes and incentives to deliver Mission Success

We align the Gemini project team with the customer team. This streamlines communication and promotes the re-allocation of workload and resources to meet changing priorities and needs. We set standards that exceed customer requirements, and we use metrics to drive performance and deliver results. We assign specific tasks and products to each staff member and make them accountable for the customer mission and program success.

Results-Focused Management: We achieve performance objectives by establishing a solid baseline; and by using processes, metrics, and standards to drive performance and achieve results. Gemini sets, exceeds, and raises performance standards to meet stringent timelines. For each task and product assigned to staff members, we set metrics, apply standards, and monitor quality and progress.

Our project baseline includes an Integrated Master Schedule (IMS), staff assignments, metrics, and standards. We use the baseline to establish accountability and to measure and control performance. We set initial metrics and project-specific standards that exceed customer requirements. And we review metrics at status meetings and adjust resources as needed.

We use our ISO-certified Quality Management System processes and procedures to foster a quality workforce and superior solutions.

- Quality Assurance processes create superior solutions that exceed prescribed performance standards. The process begins with assigning highly skilled personnel who share a commitment to excellence and continues through the delivery of products and services.

- Quality Control processes promote focused activities, consistent and predictable results, shorter cycle times, and reduced customer costs. Applying the process approach involves systematic definitions of tasks, clear responsibility and accountability, identification of key activities, and mitigation of risks and negative impacts on the customer and stakeholders.

- Issue Management processes ensure timely and effective issue resolution, and capture lessons learned to avoid recurrence. Issue management begins with the recognition of a topic, event, or action that is of concern to the customer. Issues are documented, impacts are assessed, and resolution options are developed. Lessons learned are incorporated into process improvements.

- Corrective Action processes analyze events leading up to the issue. It also covers determining defects, corrective action, and assignment of actions to prevent recurrence.

***No-Fail, No-Excuses* Standards:** We use metrics to measure progress meeting performance thresholds to drive performance.

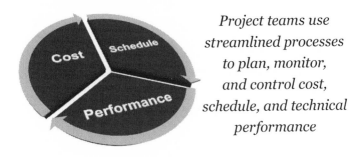

Project teams use streamlined processes to plan, monitor, and control cost, schedule, and technical performance

In addition to customer thresholds, we add more stringent internal standards to focus our actions on exceeding customer needs. We track actual results against the baseline, and work with responsible staff members to resolve issues.

We include each customer event and associated results in the IMS and identify dependencies and resources. We then assign tasks and their associated results to specific project staff and measure progress to complete tasks on time.

Zero-in on *Mission Success*

The Gemini Way uses the PARAMAX methodology to maximize the *Cycle of Success*.

PARAMAX stands for: Potential, Action, Results, Attitude—to the MAX. Gemini maximizes **potential** by assigning top performers and giving them the resources to perform their tasks. We create Results-Focused Priority-Driven Mission Plans (RPM) to focus our **actions** and accelerate progress. And we achieve **results** on the way to the BIG goals using our Quality System processes, metrics, and feedback. As we solve problems and accomplish goals, our **attitude** improves, we raise our standards, and step up to the next level of performance.

Potential: We carefully define each role on the team and select the *Best Athlete* to create the top performing team. We apply Performance Success

Indicators in a rigorous competitive process to select the right person for each role.

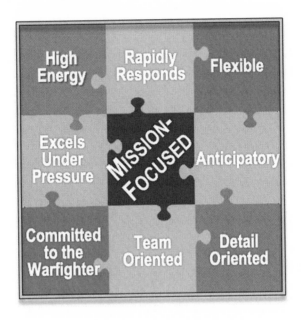

Gemini uses Performance Success Indicators
to select Best Athletes
for top performing teams

These indicators help us identify individuals who are high-energy, detail-oriented, and excel under pressure. Our process selects the *Best Athletes* with the highest potential for success.

We know that the *Gemini Family* deserves the resources and benefits that honor their talent, skills, and commitment.

Our compensation and development programs prioritize retention. We offer promotion opportunities to staff members before recruiting outside talent. And we provide comprehensive leave, insurance, and retirement plans to support the members of the team and their family.

Action: RPM focuses activities and accelerates progress. It maximizes results and channels the power of momentum to push you to *Mission Success.*

Mission Success depends on achieving outcomes. We break down each outcome into results and create a milestone schedule that ties results to milestones. Our Mission Plans focus tasks for the week, month, and quarter on the actions required to complete milestone tasks and products on schedule. We avoid activities that detract from progress and we adjust our plan to meet the changing priorities of customers.

Project teams meet periodically to discuss progress, changes, and next steps. They celebrate team achievements and recognize the contribution of members of the team. This renews the drive to meet challenges and re-focuses attention on the tasks ahead.

Results: Gemini Project Leaders track progress against RPM results. They incorporate changes in priorities, opportunities, and risks. And they work with responsible staff members to resolve issues.

As critical milestone dates approach, they determine the actions required to meet deadlines. They assess the optimal workload re-allocation, make changes to resource assignments, and closely monitor progress to completion.

RPM results must be quantifiable. For example, "10 percent increase in information reviewed and assessed in a week" is quantifiable. Quantifiable results allow us to easily confirm completion, celebrate achievements through the year, and make course corrections. We base results on key performance metrics determined by historical data. This allows us to identify changes in resources and standards that will improve customer satisfaction and enhance operations.

For example, many customers formally review product/service quality, schedule, management, business relations, and cost control. In each area, the customer documents their rating (*Exceptional, Very Good, Satisfactory,*

Marginal, or *Unsatisfactory*), provides comments discussing examples, and provides recommendations. We track the ratings in each area and use metrics designed to increase *Exceptional* ratings received. During the last twenty-five years, 90 percent of Gemini performance ratings were *Exceptional* or *Very Good*.

In Business Development, we track new business pursued and won by (1) dollar value, (2) Government agency and military service, and (3) geographic area. Using this information, we prioritize new business targets, improve processes, and identify new tools/upgrades. Since 2015, new business has increased from $7 million to more than $50 million.

Attitude: Delivering results builds confidence and brings great pride. We ignore the naysayers and the critics. We focus on the men and women serving in hostile environments. And accomplishing the *Impossible* reinforces our belief we can do it again.

Many make the mistake of ignoring achievement. It is common because they are busy working on a new threat, next challenge, or unexpected change. Gemini celebrates achievements with bonuses and awards at company meetings and special events.

Gemini's Bonus and Awards Program highlights individual and team accomplishments and recognizes their contribution to *Mission Success*. Quarterly and Annual Awards are presented within each Division to recognize top performing individuals and teams.

In 2004, I established a program to recognize unique achievements that are above and beyond those required by a staff member's position, or that can reasonably be expected. Program awards ranging from $100 to $10,000 highlight staff member actions that deliver WOW and provide another vehicle to allow them to share in the company's success.

- One Gemini staff member (I'll refer to him as Dwayne *The Rock* Johnson) developed a tool to track AF requirements and identify scheduling issues. Using the tool, he identified a shortfall and developed a strategy to save $1.2 million. *The Rock* received a $2,500 bonus.

- Another Gemini staff member (let's say Kim Kardashian) led the execution of a Simulation and Training budget and wrote and staffed a $1.5 million unfunded requirement to upgrade software and enhance training. In addition, anticipating that funds may become available, she postured the simulator acquisition community to rapidly execute actions to secure additional funds—allowing the customer to apply $2.5 million to unfunded requirements. Kim received $1,000.

At Quarterly Stock Program updates, Officers, Division Directors, and Project Managers review progress to achieving goals for the year, staff member achievements, and next steps.

We also seek opportunities to communicate how much we value each individual by having special events. Over the years, Gemini Special Events have featured singer-songwriter Edwin McCain, Olympic Gold Medalist Bill Cleary, and sports figures such as Pedro Martinez, Evan Longoria, Matt Light, and Tedy Bruschi.

After successful completion of a challenging task or customer goal, we raise standards. Delivering WOW rejects the ordinary. The team must consistently deliver the spectacular. Raising standards communicates to the Gemini team, to the customer, and to the nation that performance will always improve, and *Mission Success* will never be in question.

Intensify momentum with PARAMAX

You contribute to success by focusing your talent, skills, energy, and commitment.

You contribute to success by applying PARAMAX to your tasks. You support important projects. You are responsible for providing rapid-response, preparing quality products, and delivering priority outcomes on time. You contribute to *Mission Success* if you:

- Identify risks and seek opportunities to improve support.

- Adjust your work to meet customer priorities.

- Support your team members in meeting accelerated schedules or high priority projects.

You also optimize team performance when you tell your supervisor about progress, issues, and customer needs and assist other members of your team.

The PARAMAX methodology helps you leverage resources and focus your efforts. It also applies momentum to ease efficient completion of your tasks—and success.

Optimize Potential: As you are assigned tasks, invest time to understand available resources that would enhance or accelerate progress.

Learn the capabilities of Gemini project and customer systems and databases and get to know the members of your team. Understand and appreciate the strengths of each team member and be ready to help them in areas where they are weak.

Look outside your immediate team to other Gemini teams that support your customer and to those that support other customers. As you see resources that could benefit your tasks, contact your supervisor to request these resources.

Optimize Action: Create a schedule with key milestones and set the dates so that you accomplish each milestone three days early.

Work to complete each milestone according to your schedule. Seek assistance from your Gemini team members and supervisor as soon as you think that on-time completion might be at risk.

In addition, update progress to your Gemini supervisor one week prior to the date of each milestone. This approach will give you interim feedback, additional support, and extra time to address unexpected changes and delays.

Optimize Results: You deliver WOW with quick response and innovative solutions that are early and under budget, maximize opportunities and minimize risks, and challenge the status quo when appropriate.

Pay attention to the priorities and status of other project team members. Many times, you can contribute to their success with very little effort. You may have developed a tool that will accelerate their progress. Your idea could spark their solution. Your support will contribute to team success.

Optimize Attitude: Challenge yourself and raise your personal performance standards.

There will always be times when activities do not go as planned. You will miscalculate risks, miss opportunities, or make errors. Invest the time to find the assumptions, processes and training that could have prevented the issue. And take the actions necessary to address shortfalls and improve your future tasks.

Pursue growth opportunities within your project. Volunteer for challenging tasks. Challenging tasks improve your skills and expand both your experience and skillset. These tasks also force you to leave your comfort zone, think faster, and question assumptions. The challenge will bring excitement to your day and energy to your resolve.

Hold the line as things change

Things always change . . . many times without warning. The speed of progress is increasing; and you are nearing that result that you have been pursuing so hard. Then a sudden change forces you to stop, reverse direction, and start again.

Remember . . . you are a winner. A winner does not have the choice to quit (Chapter 5). Everyone has personal limits. But you will not fail because you quit.

Although the changes are frustrating, tasks, products, and schedules must be changed to reflect the new priorities. You know that you are not successful until the team is successful. Achieving a result that is at odds with customer priorities wastes time and detracts from *Mission Success*.

Focus your attention on the new priority. Determine if there are any tasks already started that will contribute to your new tasks and assess the time and effort involved in staying on schedule and completing your tasks.

Put extra effort into ignoring the *shiny objects*. Your customer is committed to *Mission Success*. The change in priority is not intended to disparage or harm you. The change has likely resulted from a new threat or a directive from leadership. The change probably has nothing to do with you. The time you spend wondering if the change is a criticism of you or trying to track down *Who Shot Willie* is wasted and delays your success.

What do Apple, McDonald's, and Lego have in common? They are timeless brands. These companies have built a reputation that is understood and respected by society for decades.

Your brand is your promise to your customer. It tells them what they can expect from you, and it differentiates you from your competitors.

CHAPTER 9

The Power of Perception

The explosion of podcasts, social media, and the twenty-four-hour news cycle make image important to everyone.

Although style will not overcome a lack of substance, we know that first impressions last. People often make assumptions based on a perception that is untrue and unfair. But we already know that life isn't always fair.

Perception is powerful. In Chapter 2 we described how to *Picture the Win* to gain the power to make it happen. You can imagine yourself and the world after you have achieved the goal. Your list of items (including where and with whom you live and work, and what you are motivated to do) creates a picture. You then take each step to complete the items on the list. You will create your picture and achieve your goal.

You can also use the power of perception to build strong networks and further your progress

Focus on the solution

Doing the *Impossible* is not easy. The stakes are high, and the challenges are formidable. You are tempted to study each element of the problem and look for what you can do to eliminate the element.

Unfortunately, as you study each element, new issues appear. As the number of issues increases, your confidence is diminished. And finding the solution becomes more difficult.

Instead, I picture the solution and I detail each element required for the solution. I can then determine and execute the actions to complete each element.

In Chapter 7, I discussed the threat of budget cuts to ASD. I knew that the solution was to obtain $2.5 million each year to pay for staff member salaries and benefits. To get ideas for the solution, I looked for any information that I could find on business turnaround and what makes a company enduring and timeless.

An idea came as I was watching a cable television show on Warren Buffett. I learned that the billionaire and CEO of Berkshire Hathaway began investing with commissions from his insurance business.

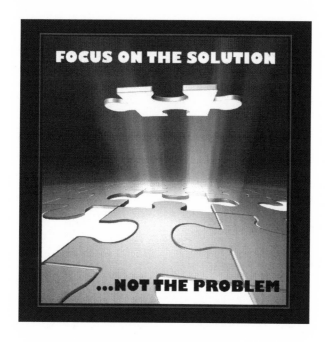

Focus on the Solution.

I knew that investing Gemini capital in the stock market could provide funds in the required timeframe. I believed that this was the best strategy to raise the funds needed to avoid salary reductions and layoffs. If investing worked for Warren Buffett, it could work for me.

Who do they think you are?

What you say can be perceived by your customer or supervisor in a way that you do not intend or desire.

Did you say, "That's not fair!"? YOU BET! Are you willing to sacrifice your success because you live in an imperfect world?

Learn the values, priorities, and needs of your customer and your supervisor. They are committed to National Security and they want you to be successful. They are responsible for specific goals and they rely on you to give them ideas, recommendations, and support. They gain no benefit from criticism, resistance, or delay. And they achieve *Mission Success* with your actions and solutions.

Beware of *Red Flag* and *Feel-Good* phrases. These phrases are common and almost involuntary. They are intended to highlight your insight and expertise. Unfortunately, things don't always go as planned.

These phrases can draw negative attention. *Red Flag* and *Feel-Good* can make you appear boastful or insincere. Even worse, you could be labelled as an egotistical person whose self-interest outweighs team goals, customer priorities, and *Mission Success*.

Put away the Red Flags: Have you ever noticed that *Red Flags* appear suddenly and without warning? They are intended to make a positive contribution by highlighting your unique and advanced skills and experience.

Some common *Red Flag* phrases are:

- Not possible . . .
- No one will . . .
- Not how we did it at . . .
- They don't listen when . . .
- They aren't . . . can't.
- That's just the way . . .

Red Flags dismiss or diminish a person, idea, or situation in order to demonstrate superiority. It is important to remember that today's *Red Flag* will become a quote attributed to you tomorrow, next month, or next year.

Everyone is tempted by *Red Flags*. Many times, they emerge while you sit there helplessly wishing that you could grab each one and throw it away before anyone notices. But all you can do is sit there, thinking, "Could everyone just pretend I didn't say that?"

Instead of using a *Red Flag* phrase, I ask a question. Instead of making a negative comment that starts with "That's not possible because . . ." or "No one will . . ." I change the comment to a question seeking information that will address my concern. I try to ask a question that begins with "How can we . . .?"

Fight hard to resist the temptation to express frustration against the imperfection of people, processes, and circumstances.

Remember how you felt the last time:

- A member of your team said to you, "That's not how we did it at my last job."

- You overhead someone describe you as, "He doesn't listen . . . He has all the answers."

- Someone told you that a member of your team said, "That's just the way it is. People complain but no one does anything to make things better."

Your supervisor, your team members, and your customer want to be successful, just like you. They can get distracted and miss the obvious, just like you. And sometimes they make mistakes, just like you.

Focus on the positive. Think about the times they showed you appreciation, compassion, and generosity. When you believe that you have an idea that addresses a recurring issue, communicate your solution in a positive way and privately.

Forget the *Feel-Good*: It is also common to use *Feel-Good* phrases when you don't know what to say. Unfortunately, these phrases can make you appear insincere.

Some common *Feel-Good* phrases are "It's a team effort . . ." and "That's just what I was thinking . . ." To avoid *Feel-Good* phrases, I think about the information that is being communicated and acknowledge a member of the team.

I might change "It's a team effort" to "Maria really stepped up to get the product completed early." Instead of saying "That's just what I was thinking," I could ask a follow-up question. And "I agree" will work in most situations.

Fly Above the Radar: It is also important to avoid the label that you are *flying under the radar*. This label tells your team, supervisor, and customer that you are not invested in *Mission Success*.

Common signals of *flying under the radar* are:

- Avoiding commitment to deadlines or results.
- Working on tasks that you think are important, instead of those assigned.
- Ignoring conflict that could improve the team.

When I think that I have started *flying under the radar*, I look for solutions. I confirm my understanding of priorities. I say what I will do and do what I say.

Highlight Symbols: Symbols have power. It is important to understand and emphasize what you communicate.

What objects are prominent in your office? Look at your desk and the graphics and artwork on the walls. Are any customer-related items or company awards displayed?

Gemini staff members supported
Oscar Night, National Small Business Week,
and the Bill Belichick Foundation.

Make sure that these objects reflect what you, your team, and your customer values. They are your symbols. You don't have to spend much time or money. You could take a cellphone photo of your team at the next lunch. Or you could print a picture from a project briefing that caught your attention. Start small. You don't have to overhaul your desk or office overnight.

Seek feedback from your supervisor. Ask if you have done well on your assignments. Ask if there are areas that need your attention. Before you conclude the conversation, confirm the new actions that you plan to take based on your conversation.

At the beginning of each week, commit to three things that you will do to contribute to *Mission Success*. Check off each item as you complete it. At the end of the week, look at the list and complete any open items before you leave for the weekend.

Seize the power

Learn the short-term and long-term goals of your team and company and look for ways to contribute to achieving them. Each year, Gemini sets quantifiable goals. We also set objectives for each quarter and month to promote momentum and progress to our goals. At Quarterly Stock Program Updates, we summarize progress and discuss actions ahead. We also welcome new members of the team and recognize the contribution of staff members to achieving the objectives of the quarter.

Focus on thinking and acting like a winner. Understand and respect the priorities, needs, and idiosyncrasies of co-workers and customers. Learn and work on the goals for the week, month, quarter, and year. Seek honest feedback and help from your Gemini supervisor.

Asks questions to understand suggested solutions. If you aren't clear on something, don't make assumptions. Instead, ask for more clarification. This will limit opportunities for failure.

Learn from mistakes by asking for suggestions and listening to constructive feedback. This is another effective way to contribute. When you receive feedback listen carefully to the feedback and ask honest questions that will help you improve.

Fight the urge to talk about why a mistake is not your fault or the failings of others. Remember . . . if the blood is rushing to your mouth, then your ears and your brain don't have a chance to give you what you need to improve.

You should also set career goals. What advancement do you seek in the coming year, five years, and ten years? You can define quantifiable objectives for each month and quarter. These serve as a roadmap for your progress. Using these goals and objectives for the month, and quarter, you can define and execute the plan to achieve your goals.

The Gemini Way encourages the career progression of each staff member. Gemini supervisors are expected to learn the career objectives of staff members, and to work with them to set and achieve performance objectives as part of Gemini's annual performance appraisal process. Gemini Division Directors consider staff members for promotion, new projects, positions, and vacancies. And as new positions at Gemini arise, recruiting teams notify staff members for consideration.

Recognize achievements in a SITREP

Create Situation Reports that include the contributions of members of the team (including your contributions) and the results achieved.

In the military, a SITREP (Situation Report) is a form of status reporting that provides decision-makers and readers a quick understanding of the current situation. Take a few minutes to create a SITREP when an important milestone has been completed. The SITREP should be brief, clear, and concise. Summarize the current status and progress made. And highlight the impact of the results achieved within the context of *Mission Success*.

Your SITREP should address the situation to date, actions completed, next steps, and issues. Keep your SITREP short and concise. And work with your supervisor to ensure agreement:

- Describe the current status including a summary of overall situation, the start and end dates of your summary, and the individuals who contributed to results,

- List the actions completed using a list of bullets or a table format,

- List scheduled/planned actions and target completion dates using bullets or tables, and

- List issues that are known/reasonably expected and acknowledge achievements of members of the team.

SITREP achievements are ideal candidates for bonuses and awards described in Chapter 8. Last year Gemini awarded more than $325,000 in bonuses and awards. Gemini also recognizes exceptional performance with Quarterly Division Awards and Annual Division, Excellence, and President's Awards and Incentive Program Bonuses.

Submit a Self-Nomination, or nominate a co-worker, supervisor, or staff member assigned to another Gemini Project. Your supervisor, customer, and leadership team within the Division and Headquarters do their best to recognize your achievements. But no one can be everywhere, and things are overlooked.

Let your supervisor know about your accomplishments so that they can celebrate with you and communicate your success to your team, to your customer, and to members of the Gemini team across the country.

Awards recognize top performing individuals and teams.

Take advantage of the power of symbols. The challenge to stand out over others is greater than ever before. Information overload and the fast-paced environment creates multiple distractions, which limit focus and progress.

You are ready to bring the power of decision, the power of momentum, and the power of perception to face the *impossible*. As you engage your resources and drive toward results, *The Gemini Way* will accelerate your progress to *Mission Success*.

CHAPTER 10

From Impossible . . . to Success . . . to the Future

Today is the day to step up to create the future and a powerful legacy.

The Gemini Way is a testament to the American Dream, and to the unique opportunity and innovation that the United States offers. It began with two immigrants who made great sacrifices to give me the values, education, support, and guidance that created the Aerospace and Defense Company of the Year and *The Gemini Way*.

My parents faced many challenges during the Japanese World War II occupation that seemed *impossible*. Almost fifteen years later, they moved halfway around the world, faced new challenges, became accomplished physicians, and raised a family.

For twelve years, we met with Immigration and Naturalization Service officials to present the documents required to remain in the U.S. My parents provided medical reports to prove that we did not pose a health risk to the U.S. population. They also brought letters from local hospitals to confirm their full-time employment and compensation.

I am sure that as my parents sat in the Immigration and Naturalization Service waiting area, they never thought that one day I would work with/for Homeland Security.

Threats will change—*The Gemini Way* will endure

What's next for National Security? Some future challenges are already known. The economy, technology, and threat will all change. Russia, North Korea, or a power unknown today could surpass China's skyrocketing economic and military ambition. Resurgence and aggression in the Middle East would not be a surprise. And the cyber threat will quickly increase, as our dependence on digital connectivity grows.

As threats change, we may have to change. But *who we are* will not change. The faces and names within Gemini may change, but *The Gemini Way* will not change.

Individuals who have been with Gemini for many years lead the next generation. Left to Right: Bradley Carriker (eighteen years), Sal Malgari (twenty-five years), Victoria Bondoc (thirty-five years), Timothy Grimes (ten years), Pedro Torres (twenty years).

The Gemini Way makes each individual exceptional, the *best of the best . . . a Winner. The Gemini Way* gives you the power to face new threats, unknown obstacles, and impossible goals.

Create your future

You have the power to create a new venture.

I know that the idea is intimidating. When I first started Gemini, contracts were scarce. The opportunity for one contract came up. The contract required me to work . . . with an Army unit . . . investigating Black Market crime . . . in a *Danger Zone*.

The Army wanted me because I had just finished working on an Air Force Command Post and I didn't *look* anything like an Army soldier. I weighed the risk of the unknown against the opportunity to contribute to National Security and decided to go. I worked with the Army for 3 months. The contract ended when the US invaded Panama to depose dictator General Manuel Noriega.

Working on the contract, I learned to create plans to limit risk. I learned to think fast. And I learned how to stay calm in a crisis. The contract increased my confidence, sparked momentum and strengthened Gemini's credibility.

You don't have to go to a *Danger Zone* to create your future. You can work with Gemini leadership to plan and pursue a new product, service, or business base. Since the start of the Gemini Stock Program, many staff members have identified opportunities to grow Gemini's business base.

Your venture could be the basis of a new business area. As discussed in Chapter 7, you can use the ASD strategy as a blueprint for creating your new Division. All you have to do is get started with a conversation with your supervisor or a member of Gemini's leadership team.

Some ventures may interfere with Gemini's National Security role. As an advisor to Defense and Homeland Security leaders, Gemini's ability to deliver products and services is limited by federal *conflict of interest* laws. These laws protect the U.S. from purchasing products or executing solutions that are influenced by the financial interest of a firm or individual.

To provide the greatest variety and in creating and pursuing areas of interest and growth,

Gemini has established a strategic partnership with Gemini MV, Inc. Gemini MV is another avenue available to you to pursue your new venture. Gemini MV pursues product and service markets and allows Gemini to avoid conflict of interest or risk.

Be proud—you set the standard

When a television program mentions *Five Eyes,* the world's oldest intelligence partnership, I think about supporting France after the 2015 terrorist attack and Gemini's contribution. When a *News Alert* reports the success of a SEAL Team, I remember the hard work involved to develop and field new combatant craft.

Although winning new contracts is exciting and expanding Gemini is rewarding, the letters of appreciation that I receive from Military Commanders and Defense leaders *and* News items on the success of projects we support, give me pride that is beyond compare.

Gemini will continue to be the standard for commitment to National Security and keeping the U.S. the Global Leader. Be proud of who you are. Be proud of what you do and what you represent. You set the standard to which others strive.

Each of you is a leader. You do not need a title to be a leader. Leadership is the gift that is given to you by the individuals within the U.S. who you protect. You must be worthy of their gift. When you are worthy of it, the members of your team will stand a little prouder and your fellow Americans will stand taller.

Each of you is a *Winner*. You set high standards, drive to overcome obstacles, and you raise the standards so that you continually improve. You know that you will succeed through hard work, discipline, accountability, and a positive team and family spirit.

You are All-In on every challenge . . . every day. You have extraordinary talent, drive, and a genuine loyalty to the members of your team, to the customer, and to the country. You are a fierce competitor who prioritizes the needs of your team and customer. And you hold yourself to the *No-Fail, No-Excuses* performance standard. This makes you unique. And this makes you exceptional.

The Gemini Team - Through the Years

GEMINI should be proud; they met the challenge; ... Yes, this was a GEMINI Victory and, thank you for allowing me to participate.

— 2018 Counter-Intelligence Project Team

Gemini has been great to me since Day 1. They have always been there for me with anything I need...I'm proud to represent the organization.

— 2007 Department of Transportation Project Team

It is an honor to work for you and I'm truly grateful for this opportunity.

— 2015 Threat Defeat Team

Although I am thousands of miles away, Gemini really does know how to make me feel close by and a part of the team.

— 2009 Seattle, WA Team

I have been at USSOCOM for over 17 years and have worked for Booz Allen, Jacobs, and ASE and by far Gemini and its management team have been the "Best" company to work for.

— 2010 US Special Operations Command
Project Team.

Melissa [my wife] commented more than once about how impressed she was with the company and the personal touch everyone displays (she used to work as a broker on Wall Street and was a financial planner, so she's seen the high-pressure only the money counts side of things) ... I'm glad to be part of it all! Thanks for having me on the Team.

— 2013 Threat Defeat Team

Gemini is a great company and by far better than many of your competitors (those that think they're your competition anyway).

— 2008 Air Force Project Team

You and your team are ready to give whatever it takes. The road is tough, and the days may become more difficult than you may expect. Only the tough fulfill their goals.

As a member of the Gemini team, you represent something *special*. Your team has delivered critical equipment to Special Operations Forces worldwide and implemented corrective action for strategic nuclear defense capabilities.

You are the *force behind the force*. You serve the men and women who sacrifice for our Nation. Your ideas, efforts, and systems are critical to our National Security leaders, as they meet new and challenging threats through the twenty-first century and beyond.

You will receive the greatest reward for your efforts—Pride that comes with the *All-In, No-Fail, No-Excuses* results you bring to the Nation.

In addition to being a *Winner*, you will have:

- **Power to increase your professional and financial growth:** Take an active role in accelerating your professional and financial growth and in achieving goals.

Focus on thinking and acting like a winner and create customer *Mission Success*. Work with your supervisor to set a career path and performance goals within Gemini. And communicate your achievements to earn Gemini Awards and Incentive Program Bonuses.

- **A family that not only supports you, but also *has your back:*** Just as you committed to supporting the members of your Gemini team, they are committed to you.

This means that although the other members of your team have an assigned role and tasks to complete, they have committed to letting you know about risks and opportunities that will contribute to your success and to supporting you and your tasks when needed.

- **Pride when seeing the results of your efforts in the news and the country:** Think about how many terrible situations were averted because of your efforts and be proud.

Much of the work in National Security is done in a classified environment. Often, *Mission Success* means that a crisis was avoided, and *nothing happened*. Because Gemini works on high-priority National Security challenges, there will be News reports that discuss the work you do.

When you hear these reports, think about the tasks you performed and take pride in the contribution of your solutions to National Security.

You deliver WOW because you look past the obstacles and see the elements that would exist if the impossible were possible . . . and if *Mission Success* were already achieved.

You demand from yourself hard work, integrity, discipline, and loyalty to customers. You value accountability and fix problems without waiting for outside encouragement or assistance. You define the path to achieve each element of *Mission Success*. And you drive forward and complete each element.

No matter how big the challenge, or how short the time, you know that your team can come up with the solutions for *Mission Success*—and you know that you will.

Step Up to building a powerful legacy

Gemini's legacy is defined by the decisions made, the actions taken, and the challenges overcome through history. Our foundation is built on a legacy of honor, courage, and commitment to National Security success. Our legacy grows with each new experience, with each previously untested idea, and with each bold action that you have the courage to take.

The Aerospace and Defense Company of the Year Award kicks off the next era of Gemini's thirty-five-year history. So many extraordinary men and women have contributed to the security of our Nation through *No-Fail, No-Excuses* execution, and innovative Gemini solutions.

Gemini teams will face challenges that no one can imagine. They will continue to deliver solutions to ensure that the U.S. continues to be the Global Leader in Technology, with the number one economy and the premier National Security capability.

You have already contributed to the strength of the country. As you raise our performance standards and lead the next generation of Gemini staff members, you strengthen National Security and the power of *The Gemini Way*.

You have the power to step up. Do what matters *now*. Your actions impact others. Choose the actions that make the biggest difference and do more. Develop your talent, strengths, and skills. Seize small opportunities and big opportunities will follow. Don't wait to make a difference because the goal is service not success.

Just as my parents gave to me the resources and guidance to beat the odds and create the Aerospace and Defense Company of the Year, *The Gemini Way* gives you the power that you need to turn *Mission Impossible* to *Mission Success* and gives you a legacy of honor, courage, and commitment to National Security.

CONCLUSION

The Gemini Way is not just a powerful tool, it is a legacy.

The legacy you leave behind doesn't start when you are gone, it starts now. It starts with the Power to Decide, Build Momentum, Guide Perception, and Succeed.

Your legacy is built by the actions you take today, and the commitment of your team to a greater goal.

That's *The Gemini Way.*

ABOUT THE AUTHOR

Victoria R. Bondoc, CEO and Founder, shares the approach that allows Gemini to face National Security challenges in *Mission Impossible: The Power of The Gemini Way.*

It is the same approach that took her from a rare disorder that left her legally blind to working with the Army investigating Black Market crime to creating a multi-million-dollar company that operates at twenty locations across the U.S. and overseas.

Victoria's leadership and the success of Gemini has garnered Special Congressional Recognition and national industry awards. She received a BS in Mathematics from the Massachusetts Institute of Technology and a MA in Computer Science from Boston University.

Her Gemini biography can be found at https://www.gemini-ind.com/gemini-is-unique/leadership.cfm.

Made in the USA
Middletown, DE
09 April 2023

28315994R00132